T0341692

# Strategic Cash Flow Management

**Keith Checkley**

FINANCE

05.08

- Fast track route to strategic cash flow management

- Covers the key areas of cash flow, from developing a strong understanding of cash flow within the business cycle and the origins of cash flow analysis to maximising cash flow efficiencies and cash flow returns on capital investments

- Examples and lessons from some of the world's most successful businesses, including Dell Corporation, and ideas from the smartest thinkers, including DuPont, Philip Kotler, Igor Ansoff, Gahlon and Vigeland and Dropkin and Hayden

- Includes a glossary of key concepts and a comprehensive resources guide

>>EXPRESS EXEC.COM<<
essential management thinking at your fingertips

The right of Keith Checkley to be identified as the author of this work has been
asserted in accordance with the Copyright, Designs and Patents Act 1988

First published 2002 by
Capstone Publishing (a Wiley company)
8 Newtec Place
Magdalen Road
Oxford OX4 1RE
United Kingdom
http://www.capstoneideas.com

CIP catalogue records for this book are available from the British Library and the
US Library of Congress

ISBN 1-84112-337-4

Printed and bound in Great Britain

This book is printed on acid-free paper

Substantial discounts on bulk quantities of Capstone books are available
to corporations, professional associations and other organizations. Please
contact Capstone for more details on +44 (0)1865 798 623 or (fax) +44
(0)1865 240 941 or (e-mail) info@wiley-capstone.co.uk

# Contents

*Introduction to ExpressExec*                                    v

05.08.01  Introduction                                           1
05.08.02  What is Strategic Cash Flow Management?                9
05.08.03  Evolution                                             15
05.08.04  The E-Dimension                                       25
05.08.05  The Global Dimension                                  33
05.08.06  The State of the Art                                  43
05.08.07  In Practice                                           63
05.08.08  Key Concepts and Thinkers                             93
05.08.09  Resources                                            103
05.08.10  Ten Steps to Making it Work                          117

*Frequently Asked Questions (FAQs)*                            127
*Index*                                                        129

# Introduction to ExpressExec

ExpressExec is 3 million words of the latest management thinking compiled into 10 modules. Each module contains 10 individual titles forming a comprehensive resource of current business practice written by leading practitioners in their field. From brand management to balanced scorecard, ExpressExec enables you to grasp the key concepts behind each subject and implement the theory immediately. Each of the 100 titles is available in print and electronic formats.

Through the ExpressExec.com Website you will discover that you can access the complete resource in a number of ways:

» printed books or e-books;
» e-content – PDF or XML (for licensed syndication) adding value to an intranet or Internet site;
» a corporate e-learning/knowledge management solution providing a cost-effective platform for developing skills and sharing knowledge within an organization;
» bespoke delivery – tailored solutions to solve your need.

Why not visit www.expressexec.com and register for free key management briefings, a monthly newsletter and interactive skills checklists. Share your ideas about ExpressExec and your thoughts about business today.

Please contact elound@wiley-capstone.co.uk for more information.

# Introduction

This chapter discusses why strategic cash flow management is an important topic. It covers:

» uses for the investor/lender/analyst; and
» the business standpoint.

"Great news – our sales have almost doubled this month and we are exploring the chance of a new contract in the Middle East!"

*CEO*

"Sorry Sir – the bank's been on the telephone – we are in an excess position over our overdraft and I don't know if they will pay our wages cheque on Friday!"

*Finance director*

Cash is the essential fuel that drives business forward – without it the business will surely fail. Cash flow is omnipresent – there is no escaping from it – whether you are the business person, the investor, or the lender. The importance of strategic cash flow management has been experienced by many with unexpected cash shortages and even occasional cash surpluses. Cash flow issues are often highlighted in sources such as the financial press.

The following are extracts from four illustrative articles originally published in the *Financial Times*, the *Independent*, and the *Daily Telegraph*. The ideas emanating from these articles led to the publication of my first book on cash flow management in 1994.[1]

The first article features the importance of cash generation and raises the issue of how the stock market assesses and rates business performance.

## CASHFLOW BECOMES THE DETERMINING FACTOR

With UK corporate finances coming under pressure in the recession, attention is focussing on companies' ability to generate cash. It is, after all, cash which pays the dividends. And since companies are essentially rated by the stock market on the basis of their future dividend potential, cashflow is a vital measure of corporate financial health.

The stock market has not in the past put much emphasis on judging companies by their cash generating ability. Analysts have traditionally assessed a company's performance in terms of a handful of yardsticks, with most emphasis put on the price/earnings per share ratio. But these measures have become less reliable in recent years, as companies have become more creative in their accounting practices. The collapse of a number of quoted companies, which from the balance sheets appeared healthy, has added to concern. As the cash squeeze on companies has tightened, many have looked to ways to conserve cash, such as cutting back on investment or squeezing their suppliers in. There have been too many surprises and companies have tested the accounting rules to the limit. You just cannot afford to take a set of accounts on trust.

This makes a company's cashflow a more important investment yardstick. As UBS conclude in a report on the UK corporate sector's favoured accounting tricks: "whereas manufacturing profits is relatively easy, cash flow is the most difficult parameter to adjust in a company's accounts. We believe that there should be less emphasis placed on the reported progression of earnings per share and more attention paid to balance sheet potential and, most importantly of all, cash."

[By David Whaller and Maggie Urry, *Financial Times*, February 22, 1991]

The second article looks at the analytical benefits of using the new cash flow statement, as opposed to the outgoing document detailing the source and application of funds. For further details of the new format, see Chapters 2 and 3.

## WHEN CASH FLOW IS KING

The point about the cash flow statement is that its more rigid format makes the bad news harder to hide. The most extreme case of this is Polly Peck. Its farewell set of accounts showed pre-tax profits up 44% to £161m. Its source and application showed funds generated from operations of £172m. But a new style cash flow statement, as calculated by County NatWest, would have shown an operating cash outflow of £192m, chiefly because of a staggering £288m increase in working capital. On the other hand,

the figure of £288m was clearly displayed in Polly Peck's source and application of funds. This suggests that the novelty of the cash flow statement lies not so much in disclosure as in presentation.
[The Lex Column, *Financial Times*, April 21, 1992]

The third article illustrates liquidity problems. Readers will see that a solution is offered in the form of a potential disposal, which would generate a cash injection.

## NTL IN CRISIS TALKS WITH FRANCE TELECOM

NTL and France Telecom, its largest shareholder with a 25 per cent stake, were locked in crisis talks last night about how to restructure Britain and Europe's biggest cable group after shares plunged a further 10 per cent yesterday. That left the company's market capitalisation at just $1.4bn (£1bn) compared with borrowings and convertible preference share debt of $21bn. Bankers said that some form of debt-for-equity conversion was virtually inevitable. A senior credit market analyst with a US bank said: "The fact is that NTL has tons of debt and not enough cash flow. The equity market is now expecting equity dilution."

The liquidity crunch affecting the cable giant, which owns networks in the UK, France, Switzerland and Germany, is thought to have ended NTL's plan to float off its broadcasting transmission business as a separate tracking stock. The plan was proposed to raise cash without giving up the cash flow from NTL's most profitable unit. Analysts said a mooted $2bn sale of the broadcasting transmission arm, which distributes ITV's signals, would not improve debt-to-cash flow ratios. But one observer noted there have been hints that NTL might sell broadcasting outright which "would improve sentiment."

[By Bill McIntosh, *Independent*, July 19, 2001]

The fourth article is fairly topical and well known to many of us. The original cash flow generation must have been questionable (although hindsight helps us all). The conclusion is reached that the Dome can never generate the cash flow needed to achieve a viable business structure.

## WHY DOME WAS DOOMED TO FAIL: FROM EARLY OPTIMISM, THE MILLENNIUM ATTRACTION HAS SLID INTO A £628 MILLION HOLE

### Who is responsible for the Dome?

> The New Millennium Experience Company created in June, 1997, is responsible for delivering the Dome cost-effectively.
> NMEC took over from Millennium Central Ltd, a company set up by the Conservative Government once it realised the private sector would not accept the risks.
> Lord Falconer owns NMEC on behalf of the Government and appoints members to the board. He sets the company's "strategic direction" and monitors its cost, content and management.
> The Millennium Commission, which includes two ministers and a member of the Opposition, monitors the value of the £628mn it has pumped into the Dome.
> The Culture Department supervises the distribution of lottery money, the commission and appointing NMEC's accounting officer.

### The decision to proceed

In January, 1997, the commission agreed to spend £200 million on preliminary work for the Dome at Greenwich, south-east London. The Conservative Government and the Opposition agreed that the commission would be allowed to receive extra lottery funds to make up the shortfall if the Dome ran into trouble. The incoming Government and the commission reviewed the project and the business plan produced by NMEC in June 1997.

On the advice of Deloitte & Touche Consulting Group, the commission voiced doubts that the 12 million visitor target would be achieved. Eight million was considered more realistic. Questions were also raised over whether NMEC could raise £175 million in sponsorship. The commission was told to prepare for a £75 million shortfall.

By July 1997, the commission accepted NMEC's business plan and the 12 million visitor target. It agreed a £399 million grant and a further £50 million loan to meet any cash flow problems.

## The Dome's financial difficulties

By November 1998, more than a year before the Dome opened, first signs of financial problems emerged. The commission demanded economies in return for cash needed to ensure the Dome was finished on time. By November 1999, the Dome had used up its £399 million grant and £43 million of the £50 million loan. Days before the Dome opened, NMEC and Lord Falconer realised there were cash flow problems.

The company had sold only £3.7 million worth of tickets, rather than the £18.9 million budgeted for. In February this year NMEC, reducing its visitor estimate to 10 million, needed more money and the commission advanced another £60 million. By the end of April, NMEC's trading income was 28 per cent lower than anticipated. It sought a further grant of £38 million, claiming that it would cost £200 million to shut down the Dome. Mike O'Connor, commission chief executive, did not believe that a further grant was value for money but a £29 million grant was made. Board members sought indemnities protecting them against prosecution for wrongful trading.

On July 12, Lord Falconer told the Culture Select Committee that the position would not be reached where the Dome was insolvent. Two days later he was told by David Quarmby, NMEC's chairman, the company could run out of money within a fortnight. In August NMEC was awarded £43 million repayable from money it expected to receive from the Dome's sale. By now, the Dome was expecting 4.75 million visitors. The grant was made to "facilitate the sale" of the Dome to Dome Europe for £105 million. The extent of the crisis was clear by August when NMEC was told that it was insolvent by PricewaterhouseCoopers, a firm of accountants, despite the £43 million grant it had just received.

David James, a "company doctor," who became NMEC's executive chairman, concluded that NMEC had been insolvent since February. It was only trading legally because its directors had a duty to do so if they believed there was a realistic prospect of getting the money to cover its debts.

## What went wrong

The original target of 12 million visitors was a "broad brush estimate" and not based on a clear vision of the Dome's content. It reached this figure without carrying out detailed opinion polls. Surveys before the Dome opened showed that NMEC were told 8.74 million people were likely to visit it. NMEC said visitor numbers were hit by poor media coverage, the decision not to allow car parking or even dropping off at the Dome and the strength of the pound. The decision to allow a million schoolchildren in free cost NMEC a further £7 million. Sponsorship income was £60 million lower than £175 million expected. The report said NMEC lacked senior staff with experience in running a visitor attraction, which contributed to its opening night difficulties. The financial management of NMEC was also criticised, with successive firms of accountants highlighting weaknesses in keeping the company's books up to date and predicting cash flow.

[By David Millward, *Daily Telegraph*, November 10, 2000]

All this reinforces our belief that: *Cash is the essential fuel that drives business forward – without it the business will surely fail.*

## NOTE

1 Checkley, K. (1994) *Cash is King*. Financial Times/Pitman Publishing, London.

# What is Strategic Cash Flow Management?

This chapter describes the place of cash flow within business. It covers:

» the capital cycle;
» the use of cash flow statements; and
» major management decision areas.

"Mr Micawber ... solemnly conjured me, I remember, to take warning by his fate; and to observe that if a man had twenty pounds a-year for his income, and spent nineteen shillings and sixpence, he would he happy, but that if he spent twenty pounds one he would be miserable."

*Charles Dickens, David Copperfield, Chapter 11*

## CASH FLOW: ITS PLACE WITHIN BUSINESS

Mr Micawber's observation should perhaps serve as a warning for today's business, where all too often we find negative cash flows. Traditionally, most emphasis has been placed on the identification of profit and loss, and the asset position of a business, in providing financial information about a business. Until relatively recently both the public disclosure and taxation requirements were served by the preparation of statutory accounts consisting mainly of a profit and loss account and balance sheet. In the last decade, however, awareness has developed amongst informed users of the need for more relevant information regarding cash flows.

This is not, however, the main reason for requiring an understanding of cash flow. Over the last 30 years, we have seen the development of an increasingly fast-moving and volatile business environment. The cyclical nature of markets and economies has made the accurate prediction of cash flows the single most important management weapon in the avoidance of corporate mishap and the controlled delivery of corporate performance.

In order to complete the analysis of the cash flow of a business, it is first necessary to develop a thorough grasp of the various components that make up the flow of cash through the business. Cash is continually needed to finance the asset conversion cycle, to enable payments to the bank, to pay dividends to shareholders, to pay taxes due, to purchase further fixed assets, and to undertake research and development. The quest to improve cash flow margins, enhance the productivity of assets, and invest in profitable growth all have in common the need for a greater understanding of the effective management of cash flows.

The last two decades have seen an increased emphasis on the reporting and analysis of cash flows to examine business performance and strategies. An awareness of the strengths and weaknesses of strategic cash flow management is, therefore, essential for anyone responsible for or involved in the process of taking decisions which are dependent on the risk profile of a given business or economic entity.

Cash flows are normally reported in a *cash flow statement*. In the US, the statement is prepared in accordance with the Financial Accounting Standards Board (FASB) Directive No. 95 of November 1987. In the UK, the statement is drafted in line with Financial Reporting Standard (FRS) No. 1 – Cash Flow Statements. In countries that have adopted international accounting standards, the statement is compiled following International Accounting Standard (IAS) No. 7 – Cash Flow Statements. (See Chapter 3 for the history of cash flow statements.)

Strategic cash flow management requires a deeper understanding of business structure and performance than can be gained from financial analysis alone. Many non-financial factors – such as products, markets, competitive position, technology, location, and the quality of management – must be considered in any proper analysis. It follows, then, that cash flow management should not be used in isolation, but as part of a more extensive business exercise.

Cash flow management allows us to draw some preliminary conclusions about the performance of a company and its investment patterns. We can also examine the debt capacity and cash generation patterns of the company. Careful cash flow management enables us properly to comprehend the current and historic performance of a business. Cash flow analysis is essentially backward-looking: the most it can tell us is "where the business is now." Forecasts, strategic plans, and budgets tell us more about the future, and the cash generation or absorption that are linked to future strategic direction.

## DEFINING STRATEGIC CASH FLOW MANAGEMENT

Cash can be seen in Fig. 2.1 as the central hub of the capital cycle. *Good strategic cash flow management will effectively manage all the items within the cash flow capital cycle.* Cash does not flow of its own accord – it can only do so as a direct consequence of management

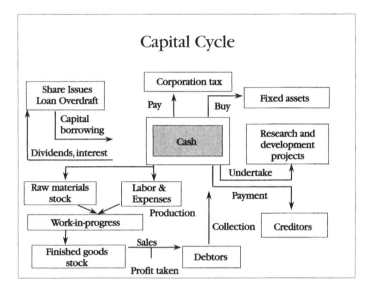

**Fig. 2.1**  The capital cycle.

decisions, taken either positively or by default. The following are major management decision areas that cause cash to flow:

» operations – these contribute to profit before charging depreciation;
» capital expenditure – acquisition or disposal of plant, equipment, or other assets of a long-lasting nature, which result in a depreciation charge against profits;
» stock – changes in the amounts of raw materials, finished goods, work in progress, etc. – increases in stock create a negative cash flow, while decreases create a positive cash flow;
» customer credit – an increase in customer credit delays cash inflow, while a reduction accelerates it;
» supplier credit and other credit terms, e.g. rent or electricity – a lengthening in credit creates a positive cash flow in that it delays cash outflow, while a reduction of credit accelerates cash outflow;

» tax – the payment dates of tax on corporate profit predetermined by law have a significant impact upon the pattern of cash outflows;

» investment – utilization of surplus cash by the purchase of investments or, conversely, the sale of investments to raise cash;

» financial obligations – interest and dividend payments, plus any contractual payments of capital arising from past financing decisions – the impact of these will determine the net cash surplus or deficit at any point in time; and

» financing – the acquisition of new money either from shareholders or by borrowing (including installment purchasing, hire purchase, or leasing to finance capital).

## KEY LEARNING POINTS

» The capital cycle illustrates the full strategic cash flows required to complete the business operations.

» Cash does not flow of its own accord. It does so as the direct result, or direct negligence, of management actions.

» Cash flows are normally reported in a cash flow statement.

» Cash is the essential fuel to drive the business forward – without it the business will surely fail.

# Evolution

This chapter traces the evolution of documented cash flow within annual reports. It covers:

» the UK/US/IAS derivation of standards of cash flows;
» the Du Pont formula;
» a review of the cash flow statement;
» cash flow forecasting;
» the use of a cash flow worksheet.

## WHERE IT ALL BEGAN

The first record of a bank lending to cover cash flow was in about 1830, when a bank financed the purchase of seed for the following year's harvest against the cash proceeds to be received from the current year's harvest – a fine example of cash flow financing.

Strategic cash flow management embraces both historic cash flow movements and the forecasting of likely future cash flows for a variety of purposes ranging from cash movement planning vis-à-vis the bank or the discounting of future cash flows to assist in the evaluation of a capital investment decision. Historic cash flows are normally reported in a cash flow statement, as detailed in Chapter 2. The cash flow statement is a relatively recent phenomenon. Financial Reporting Standard (FRS) No. 1 was issued in the UK in September 1991. International Accounting Standard (IAS) No. 7, having originally been called Statement of Changes in Financial Position, was revised in 1992 and retitled Cash Flow Statements. Prior to this, the UK and many other countries required a statement of source and application of funds in the annual accounts. This statement, whilst being a document that assisted in the analysis of cash flows, was not a cash flow statement and proved difficult to interpret and use.

Ever since the joint stock company was invented in the 1800s, it has been customary to offer shareholders an annual profit and loss account and balance sheet. However, professionals have realized that cash flows are essentially a matter of fact and are, therefore, much less prone to accounting interpretation by managers and directors of companies. Consequently, we are now seeing much more emphasis placed on the identification and analysis of cash flows as opposed to the traditional approach of data derived from the profit and loss account and balance sheet.

## CASH FLOW: LESSONS FROM THE US

There is no doubt that every business decision made will translate its way sooner or later into profitability and cash flow issues. A very useful model for examining the linkages between return on assets/profit to sales and the efficient use of assets was first developed by the US chemical manufacturer Du Pont. In 1909, Du Pont introduced a system of management control ratios for the monitoring and control of business performance, incorporating profitability ratios and the utilization of cash flow, within the context of asset investment and return. Since that time, ratio and cash flow analysis has developed into many sophisticated formats. However it is worth restating Du Pont's original formula (Equation 3.1). For readers unfamiliar with ratio analysis, please refer to the title *Understanding Accounts* in this series.[1]

$$\text{Return on assets (ROA)} = \text{(Income/Sales)}$$
$$\times \text{(Sales/Total assets)} \quad (3.1)$$

The left side of the formula focuses on profitability ratios and the right side looks at asset utilization. By monitoring performance of the key ratio, ROA, a corporate can check annual trends of return on assets and then compare its performance with corporates in similar industrial sectors. The second use is the ability to carry out a diagnostic check. By analyzing profitability ratios we can check on trading margins, and by analyzing asset utilization ratios we can check on the effective utilization of assets and the resultant effect on cash flow movements. The return on assets can be seen to be, therefore, a multiple of the profit margin on sales and the rate of asset turnover. If the overall return is improving, it must be due to improved profitability or improved asset usage, or both!

A good way of monitoring ratios is to utilize a computer-based financial analysis package. There are a number of such systems around to enable the corporate to undertake effective management controls. This is discussed in more detail in Chapter 4.

## REVIEW OF THE CASH FLOW STATEMENT

In November 1987, the Financial Accounting Standards Board (FASB) adopted Statement of Financial Accounting Standards No. 95 – Statement of Cash Flows – which requires the inclusion of a statement of cash flows whenever a full set of financial statements is prepared. The FASB pronouncement permits one of two methods – direct or indirect – for calculating cash flows. Under the direct method, the actual cash inflows and outflows associated with operating activities are presented. The new accounting rules encourage this method of presentation but also permit an indirect method of calculation that starts with net income and makes a series of adjustments for depreciation, deferred taxes, gains and losses on sales of equipment and businesses, and changes in working capital.

## The direct method

A direct method for calculating cash flows, the uniform credit analysis (UCA) cash flow statement is highly structured and reveals the actual cash inflow or outflow of each item on the income statement. Its calculation of cash net income begins with cash receipts from sales and then makes deductions for suppliers, employees, creditors, and stockholders, as well as the government in the form of taxes. With its focus on actual cash flows and its specific identification of such items as cash flow from sales activity, cash cost of goods sold, and mandatory debt retirement, it yields additional information on the structure of cash flows that cannot be found in an indirect approach. Also, its standardized format facilitates comparisons across firms.

## EARLY WARNING SIGNS OF BANKRUPTCY USING CASH FLOW ANALYSIS

A major study that examined in depth cash flow variables between corporates led to the conclusion that there were seven key cash flow variables.[2] These suggested ratios capture statistically significant differences between bankrupt and non-bankrupt firms, on average as much as five years prior to bankruptcy. These ratios and variables are thus strong candidates for inclusion in the early warning systems that we can use for identifying potential problems.

The cornerstone of the emphasis is on past and prospective cash flows, together with close scrutiny of the economic and competitive environments, managerial performance, and traditional operating and financial ratios. As noted by Malcolm Murray, Jr, former president of Robert Morris Associates, "This [emphasis on cash flow] all comes back to the fundamental premise that bank loans can be repaid only with cash." This narrative reports the results of a comparison of the cash flow profiles and selected ratios of a sample of companies that ultimately filed for bankruptcy with those of a sample of non-bankrupt companies. The comparison of their cash flow profiles is made in terms of a standardized format for the cash flow statement. Each level of the statement is compared across the two samples of companies to determine whether there are significant differences. The selected ratios that are compared are those identified as indicative of how well management has managed certain areas of the firm's operating and financial activities that are critical to its cash position.

This study differs from existing studies in at least two important respects. First, this is one of very few studies to look at cash flow differences between failed and non-failed firms. Second, and most important, this is the only major study to examine such differences when the cash flows are computed using the direct method of cash flow analysis.

It should be noted at the outset that the purpose of this study is purely descriptive. The intent is to document any significant differences in the cash flow profiles between bankrupt and non-bankrupt firms. No attempt is made at this point to build a model for predicting bankruptcy or financial distress. Nonetheless, the significant differences observed in the cash flow profiles and the selected ratios of the two groups of companies suggest that the reported results can be used as another element in the cash flow analysis process.

## CASH FLOW FORECASTING

As well as managing historic cash flows, planning for future liquidity is essential on the part of any corporate. Cash flow forecasting will require little introduction to most business persons. It's easy for the bank or equity investor to say "Please prepare a cash forecast for the next 12 months." However, the compilation of the document can be a long and arduous process.

All businesses must, of course, preserve liquidity in order to meet cash commitments to the creditors, employees, and shareholders. A good forward order book will be useless if there isn't the cash needed to finance the production of a firm's products. The ability, therefore, to be able to forecast cash movements and then monitor progress is a key requirement in business planning.

A good place to start is by completing a cash flow worksheet. If your company sells mainly on credit, then the analysis of collections will be of crucial importance. However, if you are selling mainly for cash, then more focus will be needed on disbursements. It's a question of fully analyzing the cash profile of your business and committing it to the worksheet. The issue of longer-term forecasts will be looked at later in this chapter.

From the worksheet you can then evolve a monthly cash flow forecast and predict when cash will enter and leave your bank account. You will then know when it is best to purchase new equipment, take on more staff, etc.

We can now put this into practice by looking at an example case study (Table 3.1). The example is shown for a small business, and payments and receipts have been estimated for the year on a detailed monthly summary basis. The closing balance varies between a credit and debit position.

**Table 3.1** Example company: Summary cash flow forecast for the 12 months ending 31 March XXXI.

| Month ending | Payments (£000s) | Receipts (£000s) | Net cash flow (£000s) | Opening bank balance (£000s) | Closing bank balance (£000s) |
|---|---|---|---|---|---|
| April 'X0 | 1,024 | 802 | (222) | 729 | 507 |
| May | 1,335 | 1,070 | (265) | 507 | 242 |
| June | 1,244 | 1,150 | (94) | 242 | 148 |
| July | 1,634 | 1,644 | 10 | 148 | 158 |
| August | 1,270 | 1,121 | (149) | 158 | 9 |
| September | 737 | 94 | 212 | 9 | 221 |
| October | 1,173 | 881 | (292) | 221 | (71) |
| November | 1,128 | 1,048 | (80) | (71) | (151) |
| December | 1,052 | 1,194 | 142 | (151) | (9) |
| January 'X1 | 1,038 | 1,180 | 142 | (9) | 133 |
| February | 1,004 | 956 | (48) | 133 | 85 |
| March | 808 | 746 | (62) | 85 | 23 |
| | 13,447 | 12,741 | (706) | | |

## LONGER-TERM FORECASTING

The techniques used here revolve most frequently around an annualized cash flow methodology, as opposed to using detailed monthly cash flow positions. Here we are more interested in the overall annual summary of cash movement – is it negative or positive? – based on our future strategic direction for the business.

A successful corporate manager must be able to analyze, identify, and understand the company's specific vulnerability and positioning within the cycles to appreciate the cash flow needs and suggest the correct financial structure. Three key periods can be identified in a company's life.

### The growth period

» Competitors enter
» Good acquisitions climate
» Undercapacity
» High profits
» Danger of over-trading
» Scramble for distribution network.

In this period it is important to build and maintain market share. Good marketing becomes imperative. Depending on market share, basic cash flow could be positive and financing decisions should be take in the light of cash generation.

Should the growth period be too rapid, however, there would be a constant over-trading risk, whereby any finance would be of a residual and ever-growing nature, with the corporate needing to fund overall cash deficits.

### The maturity period

» Some overcapacity
» Difficult to increase market share
» Price competition
» Falling prices
» Lower margins
» Difficult to sell companies.

In this period financial discipline becomes critical in all areas, particularly cost control, overheads, price, and credit control. The overall strategy is to endeavour to maintain market share, with a possible thought towards repositioning and diversification. Cash flow could still be negative depending on the particular industry or at best be marginally positive.

## The decline period

» Substantial overcapacity
» Fewer competitors
» Falling prices and margins
» Numerous exits
» No growth potential
» Takeover possibility.

In this period survival becomes key and cash flow is critical. The strategy now focuses on terminating, diversifying, and repositioning. The timing of the exit becomes crucial, as regulatory and social issues have to be considered, e.g. redundancies or government action.

## Using a cash flow worksheet

Whatever cyclical period the business is in, the type of worksheet shown in Fig. 3.1 can be used for longer-term forecasting on an annualized basis. The chart begins with the forecasting of the gross operating cash flow calculated from operating profit and adding back non-cash items and depreciation to give a total at line A.

Next we consider the movements within the working capital cycle: this gives a subtotal at line B for the cash absorbed within the cash conversion cycle. When this is deducted from the gross operating cash flow, this gives us the net operating cash flow (line A − B). From this we then deduct interest payments, dividends, and capital repayments due within the 12-month period to arrive at net cash flow after debt service (line C). Finally we deduct capital expenditure and taxation to give the net cash flow before finance (line D). At this point we can see whether our strategic plans have resulted in positive or negative annual cash flows.

# Cash Flow Worksheet

| | | |
|---|---|---|
| | **Year ended** | |
| | Profit before interest and tax | |
| | Depreciation | |
| | Other non-cash items | |
| A | **Gross operating cash flow** | |
| | Movements in: | |
| | Stocks | |
| | Debtors | |
| | Trade creditors | |
| | Pre-payments | |
| | Accrued expenses | |
| | Sundries | |
| B | **Change in working investment** | |
| A – B | **Net operating cash flow** | |
| | Interest expenses | |
| | Dividends paid | |
| | Long-term debt (< 12 months) | |
| C | **Net cash flow after debt service** | |
| | Other inflows and outflows: | |
| | Fixed asset expenditure/disposals | |
| | Taxation | |
| D | **Net cash flow before finance** | |
| | External finance | |
| | Increase in equity | |
| | Short-term debt | |
| | Long-term debt | |
| | **Net movement in cash** * | |

* Reconcile with source documents

**Fig. 3.1** Cash flow worksheet.

Then it's a question of balancing the cash flow. If this is negative, the balance could be achieved from a possible mixture of equity/debt and cash reserves if the business has any. Alternatively, if the business is a cash generator, then there are choices as aforementioned.

## KEY LEARNING POINTS

» Strategic cash flow management embraces both historic cash flow movements and the forecasting of likely future cash flows for a variety of purposes.

» The cash flow statement, in which historic cash flows are normally reported, is a relatively recent phenomenon.

## NOTES

1 Langdon, K. and Bonham, A. (2001) *Understanding Accounts*. Capstone, Oxford.
2 Gahlon, J.M. & Vigeland, R.L. (December 1988) "Early warning signs of bankruptcy using cash flow analysis." *The Journal of Commercial Bank Lending*. Robert Morris Associates, Philadelphia, PA.

# The E-Dimension

This chapter discusses the challenges and opportunities presented by the Internet to users of cash flow techniques and tools. It covers:

» electronic publication of annual reports; and
» the creation of an e-based knowledge centre.

# E-TRADING

The next chapter in this book concerns the global dimension, so this chapter will be confined to the impact of the Internet and intranets on matters not so concerned with globalization. There has been a huge upsurge in the proportion of transactions taking place on the Internet. As business becomes more and more competitive, we continue to seek out cost savings and speedier transactions. Transaction charges are an important element in any business, and the corporate is well advised to look for the best deal they can get, in order to maximize the return on their investment. Another e-dimension that pushes people towards online trading is the fact that the information they wish to analyze before making a buying or selling decision can be available on the same medium. This comes from, amongst other areas, information available on company Websites, access to professional analysts' advice, news-sheets, and forums where like-minded individuals can exchange views.

# ELECTRONIC PUBLICATION OF CASH FLOW STATEMENTS

Companies have been publishing accounts on their Websites for some time. In the past, this was seen as the provision of information to potential customers and investors, but it was not the primary means of communicating with existing shareholders. In December 2000, in the UK, the Companies Act was amended to allow companies to communicate electronically with their members. The annual report and accounts can now either be sent by e-mail or the information can be made available on a Website and the shareholders informed by any agreed means.

From the point of view of the major company, this offers an opportunity of cost savings on printing and postage. An e-mail sent to all or the majority of shareholders is a comparatively cheap way to comply with their legal obligation to provide annual accounts. If the accounts of a UK company are placed on a Website, they will be available on a worldwide basis. Therefore, the accounts need to indicate that they are prepared on the basis of UK legislation and accounting standards, and that they have been audited subject to local rules. As we will see in Chapter 5, the standards that companies are required to use will become more and more uniform on a worldwide basis.

## SHARING INSIGHTS AND INFORMATION

The e-dimension here is obvious, in that information recorded on the company intranet is available instantly to other people around the world. So, the technology is here. That just leaves the problem of motivating the people with the insights to share them. This is a much more difficult obstacle to overcome.

As regards cash flow information, the e-dimension allows the following two checks to be made.

1 **Comparing your organization's performance with the competition:** Easy access to your competitors' annual reports gives you the opportunity to compare their strategy and cash flows with yours. And, if you use the consistent model detailed in Chapter 10 to do the analysis, you can in this way produce a very useful cash flow comparison industry average by adding the results together and creating the average. This in turn allows you to see if the differences in cash flow performance give you any ideas towards improvement.
2 **Checking the viability of customers:** Access to information on your debtors or, perhaps more importantly, prospective debtors could avoid the risk that you will do business with a company whose finances and cash flows are thin or whose strategy is unlikely to maintain a competitive edge in the long term.

## AN E-BASED KNOWLEDGE CENTRE

There are a number of Websites available offering tools and techniques to assist with strategic cash flow management.

### Tools and techniques

There are many Websites to visit, but below are some you may wish to check out, which cover a variety of tools and techniques to assist with strategic cash flow management. Please note that neither the author nor the publisher can validate or guarantee the information bases.

## Up Your Cash Flow – www.cashplan.com

**Tools for your business:** The purpose of the cash plan online (CPO) is to provide the business community with access to a forum of professionals and other members of the business community who, by virtue of their experience, can provide information, data, and solutions to common financial problems facing the business community. Remember: The information provided here is for informal purposes only. Always consult with your professional advisors.

## TranSettlements Network
## Services – www.transettlements.com

**Revenue @ the speed of e-business:** TranSettlements has teamed with eRevenue to bring our shipper and carrier customers an innovative invoice financing product specifically designed for small- to medium-size businesses trading online. eRevenue combines the power of the Internet and the speed of e-commerce to bring businesses around the world a revolutionary new cash flow management tool, enabling them to get cash for their invoices in real time.

## Richmond Software – www.richmondsoftware.com

**Cash forecasting:** Powerful cash forecasting functionality has been built into the Millennium system. User-defined templates provide full control over the definition of the forecast categories and the time periods. Once a template is produced, it can easily be distributed throughout the organization for completion. Subsidiaries can enter their forecasts in any functional currency. On receipt of the returns, Millennium translates and consolidates this information into the base currency to provide an organization-wide forecast for analysis.

**Cash position worksheet:** The cash position worksheet offers the user flexibility for designing and analyzing future cash positions. The user can, for example, break cash items down into their constituent components to identify the underlying bank balances and transactions. Using the sophisticated filtering system with Millennium, the user can fine-tune the projections to include as much or as little of the information required for a particular forecast. These filters can be saved and reused at any time in the future.

## ISSCI.com – www.iscci.com

**ISCCI news:** Property managers secure positive cash flow with high-speed Internet access to their business properties.

## An e-knowledge base

Building an e-knowledge base available worldwide, on a corporate intranet for example, depends on growing a series of real-life projects and making cases available on a database. Taking the example of strategic cash flow management, the availability and storage in the e-knowledge base of strategic and financial analysis of organizations that are key to your own is a very useful resource. On a wider basis, the use of consistent tools in many aspects of business processes helps build a large database of knowledge, which the organization needs to maintain.

## E-LEARNING

The availability of best practice concepts and explanations allows people with access to any e-knowledge center to use a self-paced learning environment and to learn at the point of doing. The articles below are an attempt to show what can be gleaned from the Web as a means of widening knowledge and practices.

## Article 1

**Title:** "How fast can your company afford to grow?"
**Subject(s):** Industrial management; self-financing; decision-making.
**Source:** *Harvard Business Review*, May 2001, vol. 79 no. 5.
**Website:** www.hbsp.harvard.edu/hbr/
**Author(s):** Churchill, N.C. & Mullins, J.W.
**Abstract:** Reports the framework for the growth management of a company. Factors contributing to growth; determination of self-financiable growth rate (SFG); implication of SFG rate for operating management decisions.

"It takes money to make money, of course. But exactly how much money does it take to grow how much? Here's a precise way to calculate how fast you can grow a business without running out of cash.

"Everyone knows that starting a business requires cash, and growing a business requires even more – for working capital, facilities and equipment, and operating expenses. But few people understand that a profitable company that tries to grow too fast can run out of cash – even if its products are great successes. A key challenge for managers of any growing concern, then, is to strike the proper balance between consuming cash and generating it. Fail to strike that balance, and even a thriving company can soon find itself out of business – a victim of its own success."

## Article 2

**Title:** "Making cash flow."
**Subject(s):** Cash management; electronic commerce.
**Source:** *Export Today*, July 1998, vol. 14 no. 7.
**Website:** www.gbmag.com
**Author(s):** Morphy, E.
**Abstract:** Focuses on the challenges an average global company can encounter in cash management. Information on Unilever Co.'s financial system and the European financial infrastructure; information on savings that can be gained from electronic commerce; reference to the Uniform Electronic Transactions Act.

"The technology is there. But the financial and legal arrangements are just now emerging to make the most of your cross-border money. Four years ago, Unilever's top executives decided they wanted a new electronic financial system to maximize the conglomerate's cash flow and minimize its foreign exchange costs and exposures for its numerous European operations. Unilever eventually hired Atlanta-based software provider Global Payment Systems to install its Global PC-NETS electronic banking package, which is designed to link a company's accounts payable, accounting, and treasury systems to multiple banks."

## Article 3

**Title:** "Plugging in finance to complete the flow of e-commerce."
**Source:** *Strategic Finance*, May 2000, vol. 81 no. 11.
**Author(s):** Pyne, J.M.

**Website:** http://www.mamag.com/strategicfinance/

**Abstract:** Electronic commerce is reshaping the world. It has already changed processes, products, and customer expectations. Now it is joining the major elements of commerce – goods, information, and funds – into a single, converged flow, accelerated and amplified by technology. This new, seamless e-commerce flow demands that finance play a more innovative role in moving money where and when it is needed throughout the supply chain. Now the same Internet technology that binds goods and information offers a similar opportunity to intensify the role of funds along the flow of e-commerce. This opportunity is drawing non-traditional sources of capital into the financial services arena. Whether from traditional or fresh sources, financial products are needed to provide critical lubrication to the intricate machinery of the new model supply chains.

"CFOs and controllers check out the non-traditional sources of capital that are entering the financial services arena.

"Joe Pyne is senior vice president of marketing and corporate development for United Parcel Service (UPS). As part of his responsibilities, Pyne oversees UPS subsidiaries that enable global commerce, including UPS Capital Corporation. You can reach Joe at jmpyne@ups.com."

## KEY LEARNING POINTS

» The e-dimension will impact on strategic cash flow management in a number of ways, but principally in the availability of e-publications as part of the annual report, which can be immediately downloaded by investors and other interested parties.

» E-knowledge bases can be based on the corporate intranet and this will lead to a greater sharing of information and ideas.

» Tools and techniques can be found offered on many Websites to assist with both the planning and control of strategic cash flow management.

# The Global Dimension

This chapter considers the implications of globalization in terms of strategic cash flow management. It covers:

» the reporting of cash flows under UK, IAS, and US standards; and
» the similarities and differences, rather than the validity or otherwise, of each standard.

As we all are becoming aware, doing business globally is not as easy as we might think – the modus operandi of Europeans, Americans, and Asians is very different in terms of both cultural issues and business practices. Furthermore, the management of cash flow within the global context is subject to variances also.

The International Accounting Standards Committee (IASC) came into being in June 1973. In his biography, *Accounting for Life*, Lord Benson, who was the IASC's creator, said "The impact of IASC will not be revolutionary or immediate. The impact will be important in the next ten years and of dominating importance in the presentation of financial statements by about the year 2000."[1] Lord Benson's prediction has proved remarkably accurate. Recently, we have seen an increasingly powerful consensus emerge supporting the use of international accounting standards (IAS) as a globally acceptable reporting format. Recognizing this, the distinguished accounting academic Sir Bryan Carsberg joined the IASC as its secretary general in May 1995. In that month's issue of *Insight,* the newsletter of the IASC, he said that "many people had said to him that global harmonisation in accounting is an idea whose time has come" and that "a major part of the need is in the globalisation of capital markets."

Companies wishing to access overseas capital markets currently have to publish their results in a variety of accounting formats of other nations. For example, the accounts of Nokia, the Finnish telecommunications business, offer their results in Finnish generally accepted accounting principles (GAAP), in accordance with IAS, and in US GAAP. Clearly, this is expensive for the company and confusing for the user of the accounts. The disclosure of three different measures of profit is driven by the need to satisfy a variety of existing external disclosure requirements. If anything, this proliferation has highlighted the subjective nature of profit recognition as each of the three GAAP approaches yields different profit figures.

Table 5.1 outlines the accounting fundamentals and analytical pitfalls that need to be understood in order properly to assess the value and reliability of accounting information presented to the user for financial or credit analysis. The table compares UK, IAS, and US standards relative to cash flow as directed under FRS 1, IAS 7, and SFAS 95 by briefly reviewing the contents of each standard. The emphasis is on

**Table 5.1**  Summary of significant features of FRS 1, IAS 7, and SFAS 95.

| UK: Cash Flow Statement – FRS 1 | IAS: Cash Flow Statement – IAS 7 | US: Statement of Cash Flows – SFAS 95 |
|---|---|---|
| *Significant differences*<br>» The statement is based on cash; there are no cash equivalents.<br>» Cash includes overdrafts repayable on demand.<br>» Interest, dividends, and tax are presented as separate classes of items. | *Significant differences*<br>» The statement is based on cash and cash equivalents, the latter including short-term highly liquid investments.<br>» Cash and cash equivalents may include overdrafts repayable on demand in some cases.<br>» Interest and dividends can be classified as operating, investing (if received), or financing (if paid); tax is usually classed as operating. | *Significant differences*<br>» The statement is based on cash and cash equivalents, the latter including short-term highly liquid investments.<br>» Cash and cash equivalents do not include overdrafts.<br>» Dividends paid are classed within financing; other dividends, tax, and (most) interest are classed as operating. |
| *Cash*<br>A cash flow is an increase or decrease in cash resulting from a transaction. It, therefore, excludes the effect of exchange rate changes on cash.<br>Cash is defined as cash in hand and deposits with qualifying financial institutions repayable | *Cash and cash equivalents*<br>Cash flows are inflows and outflows of cash and cash equivalents; they, therefore, exclude the effect of exchange rate changes on cash and cash equivalents, as this involves no inflow or outflow. | *Cash and cash equivalents*<br>A cash flow is an increase or decrease in cash and cash equivalents resulting from a transaction. It, therefore, excludes the effect of exchange rate changes on cash and cash equivalents. |

*(continued overleaf)*

**Table 5.1** (*Continued*).

| UK: Cash Flow Statement – FRS 1 | IAS: Cash Flow Statement – IAS 7 | US: Statement of Cash Flows – SFAS 95 |
|---|---|---|
| on demand, less overdrafts from such institutions repayable on demand. There is no concept of cash equivalents. Items that would fall into that category in the US or under IAS would probably be regarded as liquid resources in the UK. Liquid resources are defined as current asset investments that are disposable without curtailing or disrupting the business and are either readily convertible into known amounts of cash at or close to book value or are traded in an active market. It should be noted that current asset | Cash comprises on hand and demand deposits. Cash equivalents are short-term highly liquid investments, which are readily convertible to known amounts of cash and which are subject to an insignificant risk of changes in value. Short-term is not defined, but the standard suggests a cut-off of three months' maturity (on acquisition by the company). Bank overdrafts repayable on demand are dealt with as cash and cash equivalents, where they form an integral part of the company's cash management. | Cash and cash equivalents include currency on hand, demand deposits, and short-term highly liquid investments (with original maturities of three months or less, or with remaining maturities of three months or less at the time of acquisition). |

investments is wider than the three months' maturity referred to in the US and IAS. Cash flows in respect of liquid resources are classified separately.

*Classification and presentation of cash flows*

Cash flows are classified and reported under the following headings:

» operating activities;
» dividends from joint ventures and associates;
» returns on investments and servicing of finance;
» taxation;
» capital expenditure and financial investment;
» acquisitions and disposals;
» equity dividends paid;
» management of liquid resources; and
» financing.

*Classification and presentation of cash flows*

The cash flow statement should split cash flows during the period between operating, investing, and financing activities.

A company should choose its own policy for classifying each of interest and dividends paid as operating or financing activities, and each of interest and dividends received as operating or investing activities. Taxes paid should be classified as operating activities unless any particular tax cash flow (not merely the related expense in the income statement) can be specifically

*Classification and presentation of cash flows*

Cash receipts and payments are classified as operating, investing, and financing activities.

Interest received and paid (the net amount of interest capitalized, which is classed as investing), dividends received, and all taxes are included under operating activities. Dividends paid are classed as financing activities.

Net cash flows from all three activities are totalled during the period, which is then reconciled to the opening and closing cash and cash equivalents. Cash flows

*(continued overleaf)*

**Table 5.1** (*Continued*).

| UK: Cash Flow Statement – FRS 1 | IAS: Cash Flow Statement – IAS 7 | US: Statement of Cash Flows – SFAS 95 |
|---|---|---|
| All interest paid, including that capitalized, is classed as servicing of finance. The statement should be reconciled to the movement in net debt, which is the net amount of debt, liquid resources, and cash.<br><br>Cash flows from transactions undertaken to hedge another transaction should be reported under the same heading as that other transaction.<br><br>Cash flows from operating activities may be reported on a gross basis (i.e. the direct method, reporting cash received from customers, paid to suppliers, etc.) or as a single net amount (i.e. the indirect method). In both cases a reconciliation must be provided separately to show the derivation | identified with, and therefore classified as, financing or investing activities.<br><br>Net cash flows from all three categories are totalled to show the change in cash and cash equivalents during the period, which is then reconciled to opening and closing cash and cash equivalents. The company should disclose the components of cash equivalents and reconcile these to the equivalent figures presented in the balance sheet.<br><br>When a hedging instrument is accounted for as a hedge or an identifiable position, the cash flows of the hedging instrument are classified in the same manner as the cash flows of the position being hedged. | resulting from certain contracts that are hedges of identifiable transactions should be classified in the same cash flow category as the cash flows from the hedged items.<br><br>While companies are encouraged to report gross operating cash flows by major classes of operating cash receipts and payments (the direct method), presenting such items net (the indirect method) is allowable in respect of operating activities. Under the direct method, the statement begins with cash from operations by source (e.g. amounts received from/paid to customers, suppliers and employees). The indirect method starts with net income and reconciles it to net cash flows |

of net operating cash flow from operating profit (whereas the IAS and US reconciliations start with net profit/income).

With the following exception, all other sections of the cash flow statement are to be presented on a gross basis: in the liquid resources and financing sections, inflows and outflows may be netted off where they occur due to rollover or reissue of short-maturity, high-turnover items.

Cash flows from operating activities may be presented either by the direct method (i.e. gross receipts from customers, etc.) or the indirect method (i.e. net profit and loss for the period with adjustments to arrive at the total net cash flow from operating activities). Although the standard encourages the use of the direct method, in practice the indirect method is usually used.

All financing and investing cash flows should be reported gross, save for the following exception. Receipts and payments may be netted off where the items concerned (e.g. sale and purchase of investments) are turned over quickly, the amounts are large, and the maturities are short.

from operating activities by adjusting non-cash items (such as depreciation) and the net change in most working capital items. If the indirect method is used, amounts of interest paid (the net amount of interest capitalized) and income taxes paid during the period are disclosed.

Under both the direct and indirect methods, cash inflows and outflows from investing and financing activities should be reported on a gross basis.

(continued overleaf)

**Table 5.1** (Continued).

| **UK:** Cash Flow Statement – FRS 1 | **IAS:** Cash Flow Statement – IAS 7 | **US:** Statement of Cash Flows – SFAS 95 |
|---|---|---|
| *Other matters* | *Other matters* | *Other matters* |
| Material non-cash transactions should be disclosed, where this is necessary for an understanding of the transaction (e.g. vendor placing or the inception of a finance lease). | Non-cash investing or financing transactions (e.g. share-for-share acquisition or debt-to-equity conversion) should be disclosed in order to provide relevant information about investing and financing activities. | Information about all investing and financing activities of a company during a period that affect recognized assets or liabilities, but do not result in cash receipts or payments, should be disclosed. For example, the initial recording of a capital (finance) lease results in the recognition of a leased asset and a corresponding liability in the balance sheet without affecting cash flows. |
| Foreign currency cash flows arising in a company as a result of its own transactions are translated at the exchange rate at the date of the transaction. The cash flows of foreign companies included in the group accounts are translated by the same method used to translate the profit and loss account of that company. The effect of exchange | Cash flows arising from a company's foreign currency transactions should be translated into the reporting currency at the exchange rate at the date of the cash flow (where exchange rates have been relatively stable, a weighted average can be used). Cash flows of foreign subsidiaries are also translated at actual rates | Cash flows denominated in foreign currencies are translated into the reporting currency using the exchange rate at the date of |

rate changes on the balance of cash (and other elements of net debt) is reported as a single-line item in the note reconciling opening and closing net debt with the net cash flow for the year.

In common with other companies, banks and insurance companies may report their operating cash flow on a net basis.

(or appropriate averages). The effect of exchange rate changes on the balances of cash and cash equivalents are presented as part of the reconciliation of movements therein.

Financial institutions may report on a net basis certain advances, deposits, and repayments thereof.

the cash flows (although a weighted average exchange rate for the period may be used). Exchange rate effects on cash balances held in foreign currencies must be reported as a single-line item in the statement of cash flows.

Banks, savings institutions, and credit unions are permitted to report net cash receipts and payments for deposits placed with and withdrawn from other financial institutions, for time deposits accepted and repaid, and for loans made to and collected from customers.

developing an understanding of the similarities and differences rather than commenting on the validity or otherwise of each standard. It is widely believed that the standards developed by the IASC are likely to become, over the next decade, the dominant global accounting framework.

## KEY LEARNING POINTS

» Doing business globally is made complicated by the differing modus operandi of Europeans, Americans, and Asians with regard to cultural issues and business practices.
» The management and reporting of cash flow are both subject to variances within the global context.
» The standards developed by the IASC are likely to become, over the next decade, the dominant global accounting framework.

## NOTE

1 Benson, H. (1989) *Accounting for Life*. Kogan Page, London.

# The State of the Art

This chapter identifies some of the key issues in strategic cash flow management today. It covers:

» the reporting of cash flows;
» an example of a cash flow statement;
» the analysis of cash flows;
» patterns of cash flows;
» performance ratios;
» capital-intensity ratios; and
» debt analysis ratios.

In Chapter 2, it was noted that the last two decades have seen an increased emphasis on the reporting and analysis of cash flows to examine business performance and strategies. In this chapter, we will look at the use of cash flow statements as a means of reporting and analyzing cash flows.

## THE REPORTING OF CASH FLOWS

Let's make a start with an example of a cash flow statement for a single company, prepared in accordance with Financial Reporting Standard (FRS) No. 1 (Table 6.1). Appended to the cash flow statement is a note in tabular form (Table 6.2).

### Net cash inflow from operating activities

What does this value represent? Looking at the note to the cash flow statement (otherwise Table 6.2), we see that there are six constituent values disclosed. The identification starts with operating profit; the next two items are depreciation and the profit/loss on sale of fixed assets which are added back. The objective is to identify the cash generated from operations. This is normally achieved by adding back to operating profit all non-cash items in the profit and loss account before the operating profit value is struck. Additional items in this class include loss and trade provisions, unrealized gains and losses on foreign exchange, and provisions in respect of acquisitions and reorganizations.

The second three items, the increase/decrease in stocks, debtors, and creditors gives us the movement in the investment in net working assets. Most businesses are constantly increasing their investment in stock and debtors to allow for the effects of inflation and growth in turnover of the business. This is usually partially offset by the increase in creditors each year, which arises for the same reasons.

So the cash generated from operations less the amount invested in net working assets every period gives us the net cash inflow from investing activities.

### Return on investments and servicing of finance

The cash flow statement of XYZ Ltd shows we have interest received, and the interest and dividends paid. Interest received is the cash earned

**Table 6.1**  XYZ Ltd: Cash flow statement for the year ended 31 March 1992.

|  | £'000 | £'000 |
|---|---|---|
| *Net cash inflow from operating activities* |  |  |
| (see also Table 6.2) |  | 6889 |
| *Return on investments and servicing of finance* |  |  |
| Interest received | 3011 |  |
| Interest paid | −12 |  |
| Dividends paid | −2417 |  |
| Net cash inflow from returns on investment and |  |  |
| servicing of finance |  | 582 |
| *Taxation* |  |  |
| Corporation tax paid (including advance corporation |  |  |
| tax) | −2922 |  |
| Tax paid |  | −2922 |
| *Investing activities* |  |  |
| Payments to acquire intangible fixed assets | −71 |  |
| Payments to acquire tangible fixed assets | −1496 |  |
| Receipts from sales of tangible fixed assets | 42 |  |
| Net cash outflow from investing activities |  | −1525 |
| Net cash inflow before financing |  | 3024 |
| *Financing* |  |  |
| Issue of ordinary share capital | 211 |  |
| Repurchase of debenture loans | −149 |  |
| Expenses paid in connection with share issues | −5 |  |
| Net cash inflow from financing |  | 57 |
| Increase in cash and cash equivalents |  | 3081 |

**Table 6.2**  Reconciliation of operating profit to net cash inflow from operating activities.

|  | £'000 |
|---|---|
| Operating profit | 6022 |
| Depreciation charges | 893 |
| Profit/loss on sale of fixed assets | 6 |
| Increase/decrease in stocks | −194 |
| Increase/decrease in debtors | −72 |
| Increase/decrease in creditors | 234 |
|  | 6889 |

from surplus cash. We would also find any dividends received from investments in this section, as these are earnings from investments where the business owns less than 50% of the shares and, therefore, does not enjoy control. It makes sense, where these items are material, to separate this cash flow item for analysis purposes. This is because the future flow of dividends from investments may be less certain than the business's own core operating cash flow.

Indeed, we also need to separate interest and dividends paid in order properly to evaluate the performance of the business, as these payments are driven by quite different factors.

» The payment of interest is contractual and may vary significantly depending on the inflation and interest rate outlook for the business concerned and the amount of interest, which is at fixed rather then variable rates.
» The timing and amount of dividends paid by the business, in contrast, is at the discretion of the directors.

## Taxation

This section is the amount paid in the financial period. In the UK, this represents the tax due in respect of profits earned in the previous accounting period. In other countries the grace period for payment of taxes due varies from monthly on account to nine months after the year end, as it is in the UK.

Note that there is no reference to deferred tax in the cash flow statement. This is because any charge or release for deferred tax in the profit and loss account tax charge is a movement in the deferred tax provision and is therefore a non-cash item. Non-cash items have no effect on the cash flow statement.

## Investing activities

This is the section where we find the value of capital expenditure made during the period under examination. The term *capital expenditure* is often abbreviated to *capex*. Where it is netted off against any proceeds of disposal, it is often known as *net capex*. Do not confuse the profit or loss on the sale of fixed assets (which actually represents an adjustment to the depreciation charge) with the proceeds of sale of fixed assets (which represents the cash received on the sale of fixed assets). A cash flow statement shows any proceeds of sale as a cash inflow in this section.

## Net cash inflow before financing

This is a key figure. The four sections above represent the cash generation and cash absorbed in reinvestment in the fixed and working assets of the business, paying taxes, and compensating providers of finance. The cash flow generated (or cash flow absorbed) is what remains after carrying out these essential activities

The net cash inflow before financing is, therefore, the cash surplus achieved from carrying out the activities of the business, less payments made to providers of finance. In the example above the value is positive and healthily so. However, a review of a variety of cash flow statements will show you that this is not always the case. This is discussed in more detail later, when we consider the analysis of cash flows.

## Financing

This final section shows how the cash surplus has been used (and, if it is cash absorbed, how it has been financed). The sum of the movements on equity, debt, and cash when totaled should equal the net cash inflow/outflow before financing.

Presentations of the financing section vary. In this case, the cash has been shown separately as the final figure. Sometimes all the movements are shown with a total, which equals the net cash inflow before financing.

## THE ANALYSIS OF CASH FLOWS

The first step to improving our understanding of managing businesses cash flows is to restate the cash flows in a more simplified format (Table 6.3). The purpose of this is to identify more easily the key information contained within the cash flow statement. This summary of cash flows contains all the key information necessary to make a preliminary assessment of the nature and extent of a business's cash flows. In order to evaluate the cash flows, we need to consider why these particular values represent the most important values.

**Table 6.3** Summary cash flow statement.

|  | £'000 |
| --- | --- |
| Operating cash flow | 6921 |
| Invested/generated from net working assets | −32 |
| Net capital expenditure | −1525 |
| Taxation | −2922 |
| **Free cash flow** | **2442** |
| Net interest | 2999 |
| Net dividends | −2417 |
| Other non-operating income/outgoings | 0 |
| **Net cash generated/absorbed before financing** | **3024** |
| Financing |  |
| Movement in equity – increase/decrease | 206 |
| Movement in debt – increase/decrease | −149 |
| Movement in cash – increase/decrease | −3081 |
| **Total movements in financing** | **−3024** |

**Table 6.4** Summary balance sheet.

| *Fixed assets* | *Operating liabilities* |
| --- | --- |
| *Stock + debtors + other non-cash* | All debt, including leasing, factoring, etc. |
| Cash + liquid | Share capital + reserves |
| TOTAL | TOTAL |

As can be seen in Table 6.4, all debt and the equity are split from the fixed assets, other current assets, and operating liabilities of the business. This enables us to see clearly what values represent the operating assets (italic text) and what values represent the funding or cash surplus generated by the business.

It is unusual to have large cash balances and large amounts of debt in the same business. Typically, we see one or the other. A business that consistently generates cash tends to have low or negligible debt and substantial cash reserves. A business that is substantially debt-financed tends to use any cash surplus to reduce debt and, if such a business is overdraft-financed, any cash generation simply reduces the overdraft borrowing element.

Cash is considered by some to be part of working assets: this is not so. All a business needs to trade successfully each night in its bank account is a nil balance. A business is solvent if it is always able to meet its liabilities as they fall due. Any cash generated above this, temporarily or permanently, is therefore a surplus to this minimum.

Trade and all other liabilities (called operating liabilities in the six-box balance sheet) represent an interest-free loan to the business, which arises as a direct consequence of trade. If the business ceases to trade, this loan has to be paid back; hence, it is usual to recognize this as a beneficial by-product of trading. Thus, the operating assets are represented by the fixed assets plus stock and debtors, less operating liabilities (the shaded boxes in Table 6.4).

Understanding the balance sheet, when it is reorganized in this way, assists us in comprehending the key elements of the cash flow. Let us consider what each of the lines in the summary cash flow represents.

The cash flow from operations (or operating cash flow), which literally represents the cash generated from the operating activities of the business, is utilized initially to reinvest in the net working assets and the fixed assets of the business. This is essential expenditure, because if a company constantly fails to reinvest in itself, it starts to age and fall behind its competitors as its operating asset investment is not being renewed at the same rate as its competitors. All businesses must also pay any taxes due on the income from their operating activities to the relevant authorities each year.

So the first part of our cash flow summary deals with the items in the shaded boxes in the six-box balance sheet above. The operating cash flow is the cash generated each period from these operating assets; the next two values represent the amounts needed to reinvest in the net working assets and the fixed assets of the business, and to pay the taxes due on operating income.

The cash available after this, often known as the free cash flow, is then used to pay interest to debt providers and, where relevant, dividends to equity providers. The remaining value is the net cash generated or absorbed before financing. This is a key figure. For a business that is not growing, it must generate sufficient cash at this level to cover the repayment of amounts due on debt principal. If there is insufficient cash available at this level, the business must improve its operating performance or raise further debt or equity to remedy the problem – or risk bankruptcy.

Where a business is a growth business we often find that the net cash absorbed before financing is consistently negative, as new capital is constantly being invested in fixed and working assets now, which will generate higher levels of operating cash flows in the future.

Managing cash flow strategically, we are typically seeking answers to the following three questions.

1 Is the business generating sufficient cash to renew its assets, pay its taxes, and satisfy capital providers?
2 Is the gearing of the business acceptable? Can the business support its interest and capital repayments?
3 Are the future cash flows of the business likely to be sustainable and consistent with the present pattern?

## Question 1: Is the business generating sufficient cash to renew its assets, pay its taxes, and satisfy capital providers?

In the first instance this appears a simple task. Either the cash generated before financing is positive or it isn't. If the business is absorbing (rather than generating) cash before financing there may be significant problems. On the other hand in many situations this may be perfectly normal. This is somewhat confusing! We need to understand more about typical patterns of cash flow before we go further. Let us consider some basic cash flow patterns in respect of a typical manufacturing business at different times in the business life cycle (Table 6.5).

## Start-up: Year 1

The new business is not yet generating an operating profit. It has commenced selling its product and hence needs to invest in working capital to build up its stocks and debtors. Trade credit is still scarce, so providing little offset. Capital expenditure is the largest cash flow

**Table 6.5** Basic cash flow patterns in the life cycle of a typical manufacturing business.

| | Start-up Year 1 £'000 | Growth Year 4 £'000 | Maturity Year 9 £'000 | Decline Year 20 £'000 |
|---|---|---|---|---|
| Operating cash flow | −10 | 1000 | 3500 | 7000 |
| Invested/generated from net working assets | −200 | −400 | −600 | 1000 |
| Net capital expenditure | −500 | −900 | −1000 | 1500 |
| Taxation | 0 | −300 | −1000 | −3200 |
| **Free cash flow** | **−710** | **−600** | **900** | **6300** |
| Net interest | 0 | −100 | −400 | −1000 |
| Net dividends | 0 | 0 | −400 | −3000 |
| Other non-operating income/outgoings | 300 | 100 | 0 | 0 |
| **Net cash generated/absorbed before financing** | **−410** | **−600** | **100** | **2300** |
| **Financing** | | | | |
| Change in equity − increase/decrease | 500 | 300 | 0 | −1000 |
| Change in debt − increase/decrease | 0 | 210 | −100 | −1300 |
| Change in cash − increase/decrease | −90 | 90 | 0 | 0 |
| **Total change in financing** | **410** | **600** | **−100** | **−2300** |

item, as the business is investing in new manufacturing facilities. The business receives some government grants at this stage. The business is financed by an injection of equity. Debt providers would not normally be interested in lending at this point, as the start-up phase of the business exposes them to too much business risk.

## Growth: Year 4

The business is now established and growing. The business is now generating £1mn of operating cash flow a year. It is still continuing to invest in working and fixed assets as it needs to invest constantly, in advance of demand, to be ahead of future capacity needs. The company is profitable and therefore pays taxes. Financing is still largely equity, although debt is used where feasible. Gearing is still low.

## Maturity: Year 9

The market in which the business operates becomes mature and growth in turnover slows. The business is by now making an operating cash flow of £3.5mn. Investment in working assets is still required but at a much lower rate than in the growth phase. The investment in working assets is now mainly required to compensate for the effects of inflation on the business. Capital expenditure decreases as the company is now only replacing old and obsolete machinery. Taxes increase, as there is less offset effect from capital expenditure allowances. The company is now using debt where possible, so is making an increasing interest payment each year. It pays out an increasing dividend each year because it is no longer growing in order to maintain equity returns at an acceptable level.

The business is now generating a surplus at the cash generated/absorbed before financing line and this is used to repay debt. Any temporary need to spend more than was generated would normally be financed by borrowing, if the business had available borrowing capacity.

## Decline: Year 20

Businesses in decline are rarely observed in the real world. Managers will usually change the markets in which the business operates, or the overall strategy of the business, in an effort to regain growth opportunities. However, it is important to understand the effects of decline on the pattern of a business's cash flows.

The business is now generating £7mn in operating cash flow a year. As turnover is declining, the need for working assets is also declining in direct proportion. The reduction in stock and debtors is being used to finance the reduction in operating liabilities and is still generating a cash surplus. The capital expenditure is more than offset by the cash flows generated from selling plant and surplus property as the business downsizes. Taxes are high as there is no capital expenditure offset and capital gains tax is paid on the disposal of properties in addition to corporate taxes.

The business pays high dividends and is retiring capital by annual share buy-backs; the remaining surplus is going in debt repayment.

## Patterns of cash flows

The four patterns of cash flows, described above, represent typical patterns of cash flows for a business at different times in the business life cycle. So the first key question we need to ask, before we can properly evaluate the cash flows of a business with which we are unfamiliar is, "At what stage is this business in its company life cycle?"

The vast majority of businesses examined fall into two of the four patterns described above. These are the *mature* (low- or nil-growth) business and the *growth* business. We will now cover these two patterns in more detail, starting with the mature business (Table 6.6).

**Table 6.6** The mature business.

|  | Mature Year 9 £'000 |
| --- | --- |
| Operating cash flow | 3500 |
| Invested/generated from net working assets | −600 |
| Net capital expenditure | −1000 |
| Taxation | −1000 |
| **Free cash flow** | **900** |
| Net interest | −400 |
| Net dividends | −400 |
| Other non-operating income/outgoings | 0 |
| **Net cash generated/absorbed before financing** | **100** |
| Financing |  |
| Change in equity – increase/decrease | 0 |
| Change in debt – increase/decrease | −100 |
| Change in cash – increase/decrease | 0 |
| **Total change in financing** | **−100** |

In the long run, a mature business has to be cash-positive before financing. It can have one or, possibly, two years of negative cash generation, due to temporary or one-off factors impacting on the business. Further years of negative cash flows imply significant problems with the business. Each of the years of negative cash generation requires an increase in financing.

If the company had substantial cash reserves when it entered the period of poor performance, this will usually be utilized to try and solve the problems and achieve a recovery. If the business is quoted and making low profits or losses, it will be expensive to raise equity as the share price is likely to be depressed. If the business is unquoted, it is usually impossible to raise further equity in a situation where results are poor. If further cash is required, it will therefore have to come from an increase in debt, if the business has further debt capacity available.

Finally, if the business has run out of all other avenues to further cash, it will take further credit from its trade creditors and defer payment of other operating liabilities. All this will reflect in the cash flow statement as it happens.

From this follows the question: "Is the business cash-positive?" And a further question: "Does the cash surplus appear sufficient to cover its financing obligations and any other strategic objectives the company may have?" If the answer to these two questions is yes, then we appear to have a healthy business. Bear in mind that this is a tentative conclusion, because financial analysis should not be used in isolation from other assessment techniques, such as analysis of business strategy and competitive positioning. A cash-positive business can still make strategic errors that leave it severely cash-negative in a later accounting period.

If the business is not cash-positive, further analysis is then required to attempt to establish the cause. The three most likely causes are:

1 insufficient generation of operating cash flow to support the existing levels of fixed and working asset investment and taxes due;
2 excessive debt funding costs, causing a cycle of ever-more lending and refinancing to repay existing debt, and usually resulting in the collapse of the group; and
3 lack of control over working assets, resulting in them absorbing far more of the available cash flow than was planned for.

The mature business represents the most straightforward case to examine. Analysis and assessment of the growth business (Table 6.7) is more complex.

**Table 6.7**   The growth business.

|  | Growth £'000 | Restated no growth £'000 |
| --- | --- | --- |
| Operating cash flow | 1000 | 1000 |
| Invested/generated from net working assets | −400 | −200 |
| Net capital expenditure | −900 | −300 |
| Taxation | −300 | −350 |
| **Free cash flow** | **−600** | **150** |
| Net interest | −100 | −100 |
| Net dividends |  |  |
| Other non-operating income/outgoings | 100 | 0 |
| **Net cash generated/absorbed before financing** | **−600** | **50** |
| Financing |  |  |
| Change in equity – increase/decrease | 300 | 0 |
| Change in debt – increase/decrease | 210 | −50 |
| Change in cash – increase/decrease | 90 | 0 |
| **Total change in financing** | **600** | **−50** |

Growth businesses, unless they enjoy unusually high profitability, are usually cash-negative, both before and after paying interest and dividends. This is because the business is investing in new fixed and working assets, which will generate their operating cash flow in future years. It is an impossible task to judge from the figures as stated whether the rate of cash generation is adequate to sustain the business at the point where its market and performance mature and it turns into a low- or nil-growth company.

The method we, therefore, use is to restate the published cash flows as what we think they might be if the business stopped growing. This necessitates a number of adjustments to the disclosed data. This is known as the restatement of the cash flows on a *no-growth* basis.

The first and usually most substantial adjustment is to reduce the existing net capital expenditure value to take out the growth-related component. The net capital expenditure consists of two components. First, the expenditure required to maintain existing fixed assets is what we call the *replacement* or *maintenance capex*. Second, the expenditure representing an investment in new projects or developments is known as *investment* or *growth capex*.

Although it is not a reporting requirement, some companies now disclose this split, which is obviously of great assistance to the analyst. Where no disclosure is present, the analyst must develop an estimate. In the absence of better data, the best proxy figure for the replacement capex is the depreciation charge for the year. This figure is likely to understate the true replacement value: it is tempting to add a loading for the effect of inflation on the replacement value of fixed assets. However, as we don't know by how much it should be adjusted, it may be better not to adjust the depreciation value at all.

The second adjustment is to take out the growth-related element in the investment in net working assets. Again, there are two components to this figure as disclosed. First, there is the investment in net working assets required to compensate for the effects of inflation on the existing net working assets. Second, there is the additional investment made to put working capital in place for growth reasons.

The third adjustment is to increase the tax charge slightly. This is necessary to reflect the effect on the tax charge of lower capital expenditure. In most economies, capital expenditure attracts tax allowances, which have the result of lowering the tax charge in the year of acquisition of the assets.

## Question 2: Is the gearing of the business acceptable? Can the business support its interest and capital repayments?

In order to answer this question we need to use the same technique that we have just learned about. We need to restate the cash flows so that we can examine the extent to which they cover interest and principal due (Table 6.8). In both cases we are interested in the no-growth scenario, as the purpose of debt analysis is to examine what the situation would be in a worst-case scenario. Remember that the

**Table 6.8**   The growth business: no-growth scenario.

|  | Growth Year 4 £'000 | Restated no growth £'000 |
|---|---|---|
| Operating cash flow | 1000 | 1000 |
| Invested/generated from net working assets | −400 | −200 |
| Net capital expenditure | −900 | −300 |
| Taxation | −300 | −350 |
| **Free cash flow** | **−600** | **150** |
| Net interest | −100 | −100 |
| Net dividends |  |  |
| Other non-operating income/outgoings | 100 | 0 |
| **Net cash generated/absorbed before financing** | **−600** | **50** |
| Financing |  |  |
| Change in equity - increase/decrease | 300 | 0 |
| Change in debt - increase/decrease | 210 | −50 |
| Change in cash - increase/decrease | 90 | 0 |
| **Total change in financing** | **600** | **−50** |

growth cash flows mask whether the cash generation of the business is adequate to cover the situation when the growth ceases.

So our method is to restate the cash flows in terms of the extent to which the free cash flows cover the principal and interest (Table 6.9). As can be seen by comparison with the earlier example, the inclusion of the debt principal due for repayment reveals that in a no-growth situation the business will not be generating sufficient capital to service the principal repayment from its own resources. If this situation continues the business will end up bankrupt. Two solutions are available. If the business has further debt capacity available, it can borrow more money (essentially using new money to repay old). However, this solution is obviously temporary as the business is still not generating sufficient cash to achieve break-even debt service. The second option is to improve the operating cash flow in some way: in a beneficial economic environment this may be possible, but in a recession it is unusual to succeed in achieving such an increase.

**Table 6.9** The growth business: the no-growth scenario ultimately spells bankruptcy.

|  | Growth Year 4 £'000 | Restated no growth £'000 |
|---|---|---|
| Operating cash flow | 1000 | 1000 |
| Invested/generated from net working assets | −400 | −200 |
| Net capital expenditure | −900 | −300 |
| Taxation | −300 | −350 |
| **Free cash flow** | **−600** | **150** |
| Net interest | −100 | −100 |
| Debt principal due | −200 | −200 |
| Other non-operating income/outgoings | 100 | 0 |
| **Surplus or deficit after debt financing** | **−800** | **−150** |

## Question 3: Are the future cash flows of the business likely to be sustainable and consistent with the present pattern?

The extent to which a company is capable of delivering a settled and consistent financial performance is not assessable from financial analysis alone. To arrive at any meaningful judgement about this issue, it is necessary to perform a detailed evaluation of the strategy and competitive positioning of the business and the extent to which it enjoys sustainable competitive advantages.

Financial analysis looks into the past and takes no account of the external environment in which the business operates. It follows that financial analysis should never be used in isolation. The second point to note is that cash flow statements show inherently more volatility in the values disclosed than a profit and loss account, as there are no opportunities for provisioning or profit-smoothing by manipulation of the elements of the statement. Thus while a profit and loss account may possibly show a steadily growing and successful performance, the cash flow statement is likely to appear more volatile in its content.

## PERFORMANCE RATIOS

The following four ratios (expressed as equations) should yield useful data to help us manage our cash flows, particularly if compared with long-term average values from peer group companies in the sector of the business being examined. As cash flow statements are a relatively novel phenomena, there is limited data available to make comparisons against. It will, therefore, probably be necessary for you to extract the information yourself from peer group performers.

The ratio in Equation 6.1 looks at the cash generated as a percentage of sales and can be used as an effective forecasting tool.

Operating cash flow to sales % = Operating cash flow/Total sales

$$(6.1)$$

The ratio in Equation 6.2 compares the cash generated from operations with the total investment in the business – hence we can monitor how effectively we are utilizing our cash investments.

Operating cash flow to operating assets %

= Operating cash flow/Operating assets       (6.2)

This is the cash flow equivalent of operating profit to operating assets, but should be higher as operating profit is stated after depreciation, whereas operating cash flow ignores depreciation. Again, this is a ratio to compare with competitors and sector norms.

The ratio in Equation 6.3 looks at the net cash flow returns on a free cash flow basis that are being achieved on sales. This again will be a useful tool in forecasting added value.

Free cash flow to sales % = Free cash flow/Total sales       (6.3)

The ratio in Equation 6.4 has no direct comparative in the profit and loss account. It allows us to compare the net cash generation from the business before financing costs with the operating assets.

Free cash flow to operating assets %

= Free cash flow/Operating assets       (6.4)

## CAPITAL-INTENSITY ANALYSIS

The following ratios (again expressed as equations) can be used to examine the nature of the capital investment in the business. Two of the ratios are derived from the balance sheet. They are included here as they form part of the overall analysis.

The ratio in Equation 6.5 tells us whether the business is investing at a rate higher than the depreciation charge or not. A result under 1 shows the business may be underinvesting. A result over 1.5 shows the business is investing aggressively and this should reflect in the growth rates being achieved.

Gross capex to total annual depreciation

= Gross capex/Total annual depreciation            (6.5)

The ratio in Equation 6.6 tells us about the age of the fixed assets of the business. A result of 2 or 3 is typical for a young, fast-growing business where the assets are all relatively new. A result of 8 or 9 suggests that the assets are old and almost completely depreciated.

Accumulated depreciation to total annual depreciation

= Accumulated depreciation/Total annual depreciation     (6.6)

The following is a capital expenditure cover ratio (Equation 6.7). It tells us the number of times ($x$) the capex could be covered from operating cash flow. In a capital-intensive business, we would expect a low value as the business has to continually invest substantial amounts of capital each year in order to remain competitive. In a low-capital business we would expect higher values.

Operating cash flow to gross capex $x$

= Operating cash flow/Gross capex            (6.7)

The ratio in Equation 6.8 gives us some indication whether the cash generation of the business is sufficient to increase the capex, should this be necessary for competitive reasons. It is only indicative because the business also has to service capital providers from the free cash flow.

Free cash flow to gross capex $x$ = Free cash flow/Gross capex  (6.8)

## DEBT ANALYSIS RATIOS

The ratio in Equation 6.9 can be a good indicator of whether a business is exceeding its debt capacity values. Under 5 suggests there may be problems with debt repayment.

Operating cash flow to total debt yrs

= Operating cash flow/Total debt  (6.9)

The ratio in Equation 6.10 is similar to the preceding ratio; the free cash flows represent the fund available to service all capital providers. The problem with this ratio is that for many growth businesses the free cash flow is a negative value so rendering the ratio useless. It only yields useful data for mature businesses with steady cash flows.

Free cash flow to total debt = Free cash flow/Total debt  (6.10)

If we take the trouble to restate the cash flows in order to identify this value, this will give us the best information as to the existing debt service position (Equation 6.11). Bear in mind that the ratio can easily give misleading results if the cash flows do not represent a typical year. Also, the rate of growth in operating cash flow will have a substantial effect on future debt service capacity.

Cash flow available to service principal to total debt

= Cash flow available to service principal/Total debt  (6.11)

### KEY LEARNING POINTS

> We have examined thoroughly a cash flow statement and its constituent parts, together with a number of cash flow based ratios, to assist us with performance analysis and the funding of future business growth.

# In Practice

This chapter draws conclusions from practice with case studies. It covers:

- » a study of key cash flow actions by the Dell Corporation;
- » a study of strategic cash flow management within project finance;
- » a comparative study of the cash flow statements of AG Barr and JN Nichols (Vimto);
- » capital investment payback criteria; and
- » additional cash flow management.

## CASE STUDY 1: DELL COMPUTER CORPORATION

For our first case study, let's cross the Atlantic and pick up Dell Corporation of the US. The business was achieving growth but how could this be best managed in terms of cash flow? Russ Banham reported in the December 1997 issue of *CFO Magazine* that Dell's cash flow was the subject of close involvement by the corporate treasurer and the CFO. Readers will see some dramatic results.

"In the here-today, gone-tomorrow business of computers, speed saves. Nobody knows that better than Tom Meredith of Dell Computer Corp. Since taking the CFO position at the Round Rock, Texas based company in 1993 – a job the former treasurer of Sun Micosystems Inc. nearly rejected because of the monumental challenge – Meredith has made velocity his mantra, and liquidity improvement his personal crusade. 'I've always been grounded in the belief, right or wrong, that a company's focus on cash flow has nothing but a good impact on its operating performance,' he says.

"Dell's finance re-engineering effort was born of necessity in late 1995. The company's inventories were ballooning, accounts receivables were rising faster than its revenue growth rates, and asset management was undermined by several quarters of lackluster performance. Meredith notes 'We needed to take the weight off the growth pedal and shift our focus to liquidity and profitability.'

"'We sent out a consistent message to everyone to focus on three things – asset management, return on invested capital, and cash conversion.' Speed is of the essence. 'Basically, we focussed on ways to convert what we sell directly to the marketplace as quickly as possible into cash,' says Danny Caswell, manager of Dell's asset management department. To do that, Dell went its own way, involving everyone from employees to suppliers to vendors to customers."

To determine improvements in return on invested capital, Dell's asset management team developed a set of internal benchmarks (Equation 7.1). Metrics included days sales outstanding (DSO), days sales in inventory (DSI), and days payables outstanding (DPO). Add

DSO and DSI, then subtract DPO and you get the chief metric Dell uses to measure its liquidity: CCC (cash conversion cycle).

$$DSO + DSI - DPO = CCC \qquad (7.1)$$

The metrics tell a compelling tale. Dell's cash conversion cycle went from an acceptable 40 days to a phenomenal minus 5 days in the fourth quarter of 1997. "Our biggest improvement was in the inventory area, which we drove down from 30-plus days to 13 days," Caswell says. "We analyzed key inventory drivers to identify who was holding inventory and where. It turned out to be us almost exclusively."

## Shorter receivables, longer payables

Improved inventory cycles were just part of the CCC turnaround. DSO was pared from an already respectable 42 days to 37 days over the one-year period. What did the trick? New collection tools provided to Dell's customer financial services department to improve order processing and collection activities. Dell also was able to make similar headway in the DPO metric, which increased from 33 days to 54 days. "We were often paying our bills before the negotiated terms," Caswell recalls.

### SNAPSHOT
#### Treasury operations
**Company:** Dell Computer Corp., Round Rock, Texas
**Business:** Computer manufacturer
**Revenues:** (1996): $7.7bn
**No. of employees:** 14,000

#### Best practices
1 Balanced priorities of liquidity, profitability, and growth by emphasizing return on invested capital and reduced cash conversion metrics.
2 Invited employees, suppliers, vendors, and customers into its educational campaign to develop cash conversion strategies.

3 Designated its asset management team responsible for re-engineering the financial services training curriculum to improve functions and reduce errors in order processing and collections.

4 Centralized the treasury function for domestic and foreign operations.

5 Made business units fully responsible for credit and collections processes.

6 Developed systems to improve vendor processing, customer processing, and accounting processing in tandem with the re-engineering of treasury operations.

| Key metrics | LQ4 1996 | LQ4 1997 |
|---|---|---|
| Days sales outstanding | 42 | 37 |
| Days sales in inventory | 31 | 13 |
| Days payables outstanding | 33 | 54 |
| Cash conversion cycle (days) | 40 | −5 |

Source: Dell Computer Corp.

## Dell case

Some concluding comments. You can see from the case, the initial problems were with cash management. The large amounts of cash flow tied up within the working capital cycle were causing huge problems. When you link this to the expanding sales profile, the cash conversion cycle was long at 50 days. But by introducing the best strategic cash flow management practices stated in the chart, you can see the vast improvement with cash conversion moving to a minus-5-day position. In other words they reversed from being a cash consumer within the working capital cycle, to actually being a cash generator!

## CASE STUDY 2: ABC HOTEL

### Strategic cash flow management within project finance

When we build a hotel or a power station or any type of large infrastructure project, cash flow will be key as the source of debt repayment and dividend payments to the sponsors and other shareholders. The risks inherent in project finance include the following.

» The initial feasibility: the risks at this stage are borne by the equity sponsors.
» The construction period: this is still a high-risk period. Project finance lenders will endeavor to shift the completion risk to technically and financially reliable sponsors/contractors, as well as the responsibility for cost overruns.
» The operational period: project finance lenders will have to rely on the underlying cash flows from the project and associated contractual arrangements during this stage.

Now we move geographically to the Middle East – in fact to Beirut, where the project is to build a 253-bedroom hotel called the ABC Hotel at a total cost of $4mn. The debt request is for a loan of $30mn. As we mentioned earlier, the project will revolve around cash flow. In the early stages the cash flow for construction will need careful monitoring to keep a watch out for cost overruns and so on. But later, when the hotel finally opens, the cash flow will be key to ensure debt repayments and dividends.

A financial model needs to be built to demonstrate the operational budgets and cash flow implications. Both Lotus and Excel are extremely useful packages to do this. The model that follows is not intended to be the complete answer. However, it does give an indication of how you can look in detail at the cash flows in this way and then test them to make sure they will meet the lenders' cash flow covenants by way of possible stipulated cash flow coverage ratios.

### The brief

Here is the brief for the ABC hotel.

» You have been called in, as cash flow specialists, to develop a cash flow assessment model using Excel.
» You must input the developers' figures for the hotel project, detailing the projected operating revenues and expenses over the period from 1996 to 2002.
» The proposed $30mn loan at 11% will attract interest payments of $3300 in 1996, $3300 in 1997, $3271 in 1998, $3238 in 1999, $3128 in 2000, $2941 in 2001, and $2721 in 2002, with capital repayments planned as commencing in 1997 (figures in 000s).
» Annual capital repayments from 1997 to 2002 will be, respectively, $260, $300, $1000, $1700, $2000, and $2240 (figures in 000s).
» You need to develop two cash flow coverage ratios to illustrate that the debt can be serviced.
» Finally, you are required to run some risk-sensitizing profiles of differing levels of hotel performance.

## The background

The bank has been asked to provide a secured construction loan of $30mn in order to construct and operate a five-star luxury hotel, at a beach area within 50 minutes' travelling time of Beirut.

The developers will be a special-purpose company, established for the project. They have appointed a local company, Consultancy (PVT) Limited, to undertake the construction and management of the project. We understand that they have considerable expertise in the construction of deluxe hotels and that they have been closely involved with the design and planning of the hotel.

The bank will appoint an independent firm of quantity surveyors to monitor the construction on their behalf, and the monthly reports will be monitored by a leading firm of accountants.

## The project

The project will comprise a 253-bed, five-star hotel located on the coast. The site is located some 50 minutes' drive from the capital. The site covers an area of 8 hectares, bordered by beachfront on the western side, and also contains a freshwater lagoon to the south. We understand that there are no problems regarding the site, such as flooding or any serious underground conditions.

The developers have been granted a lease to the land by the government for a 20-year period from August 16, 1995, with a further four 10-year periods of renewal. The initial rent is $8560 in the first year, rising to $15,360 in the twentieth year. The lessor has the right to cancel the interest, should the land be required for public purposes. However two years' notice must be given, together with compensation. Tourism is a major source of foreign exchange earnings and a key generator of employment.

The developers have identified a strong demand for a luxury-class, resort-based hotel. The demand for hotel rooms is dominated by European travellers (62% of all travellers).

## Future hotel supply and demand

In addition to the hotel, we understand that there are a number of other hotels in the pipeline. However, these are three-star properties and the bank's hotel division has identified a projected supply of 1809 rooms in first-class hotel accommodation over the next five years (Table 7.1).

**Table 7.1**    Present and future hotel project supply.

| | |
|---|---:|
| Projects under construction (of which this project comprises 253) | 1809 |
| Approved projects (i.e. with planning) | 904 |
| | 2713 |
| Proposed or "rumoured" projects, but not approved | 990 |
| Total | 3703 |

The demand for hotel accommodation has been identified by the bank's hotel division, because maximum occupiers have typically achieved levels well over 90%. Furthermore, there is a growing demand worldwide for luxury-resort holidays, particularly in those hotels operated by the leading hotel chains.

## Construction

Detailed plans and drawings have yet to be provided. However, initial cost appraisals have been examined and the project will cost approximately $41mn or approximately $160,000 per room. The resort will be in the traditional style, comprising clusters of rooms with private terraces, as well as offering a full range of facilities.

## Operating levels

The bank's hotel division has undertaken thorough on-site research and has taken a conservative view of occupancy and the room rate, which reflects the increased competition as a result of the increases in hotel supply. These figures have formed the basis of the valuation figures.

The bank's hotel division has proposed a conservative level of occupancy for the first six years from 1996 (Table 7.2).

**Table 7.2** ABC Hotel: Projection of occupancy level and room rate in the six-year period from 1996.

| Years | 1 | 2 | 3 | 4 | 5 | 6 |
|---|---|---|---|---|---|---|
| Occupancy % | 55 | 61 | 58 | 62 | 68 | 68 |
| Average room rate ($) | 195 | 225 | 245 | 270 | 284 | 298 |

## Valuations

This appraisal considers the intrinsic land value attributable to the site, as well as the net completed value of the project on completion in 1996. We have three sets of valuations for each, prepared by independent chartered surveyors.

1 Land value: The consideration paid for the site was $678,645. Two of the valuers provided evidence of recent land transactions, and their opinion of land value ranged between $1.47mn and $1.86mn. In our view, the value of the land at today's prices is $1.47mn.
2 Completed value of hotel resort: The valuations of the completed project have been based upon the occupancy levels projected by the developers' advisors, which are less conservative than the bank's. The valuations have been based on a range of capitalization rates. A comparison of the valuations is shown in Table 7.3.

**Table 7.3** ABC Hotel: Comparison of valuations of the completed project, based on the hotel opening in 1996.

| | |
|---|---|
| Estate agent (Beirut office) | $60mn |
| Surveyor (based in location) | $48.07mn |
| Surveyor (based in Beirut) | $45mn |

The construction budget (Table 7.4) shows the planned outgoings in stages to reach a total of $43.2mn, including the expected interest charges.

This is a start of the financial model (Table 7.5). We begin with the top-line inputs from the expected occupancy levels and room rate charges. In 1996 for example, with food and other incomes, we generate a total revenue line of $17.565mn and deductions of operating expenses of $8.205mn. In this type of project, it is then useful to give departmental contribution streams: these are stated and total $9.36mn. You can then work your way down the figures and see we arrive at an EBIT (earnings before interest and tax) of $4.28mn.

To derive the cash flow in terms of hotels we can take the EBIT and add back any non-cash items such as depreciation and amortization to arrive at a term known as EBITDA. This is a term frequently used by American analysts and is often included in a lender's term loan documentation in setting cash flow covenants.

Returning to the ABC hotel at the bottom of the model, we have added two cash flow ratios (Equation 7.2 and Equation 7.3). Based on the input assumptions in terms of occupancy levels and room rates, the cash flow ratios indicate that the debt can be serviced and interest payments covered.

$$\text{Cash flow interest cover} = \text{EBITDA/Interest} \tag{7.2}$$

$$\text{Debt service ratio} = \text{EBITDA/Interest and capital repayments} \tag{7.3}$$

## "What if?" scenario

The next step is to run a sensitivity analysis and this is where software such as Excel is a great help. Provided you link the various inputs mathematically to the financial model data, e.g. occupancy levels and

**Table 7.4** ABC Hotel: Construction budget (note: all figures in 000s).

| | 1 | 2 | 3 | 4 | 5 | 6 | 7 | 8 | 9 | 10 | 11 | 12 | 13 | Total |
|---|---|---|---|---|---|---|---|---|---|---|---|---|---|---|
| Land | 678 | | | | | | | | | | | | | 678 |
| Construction | 1,824 | 1,000 | 1,000 | 1,800 | 1,803 | | | | | | | | | 7,427 |
| Equipment | 200 | 600 | 800 | 800 | 800 | 800 | 800 | | | | | | | 4,800 |
| Interior work | 150 | 750 | 1,000 | 1,250 | 1,250 | 600 | 600 | 500 | 466 | | | | | 6,566 |
| Plumbing/treatment plant | 300 | 1,500 | 1,000 | 1,250 | 1,250 | 400 | 400 | 400 | 286 | | | | | 6,786 |
| Swimming pool | | 200 | 500 | 500 | 500 | 300 | 300 | 178 | | | | | | 2,478 |
| Landscaping | 100 | | 100 | 300 | 300 | 300 | 300 | 110 | | | | | | 1,510 |
| Marketing and opening fees | | 434 | | | 74 | 388 | | 272 | | 155 | 974 | | | 2,297 |
| Professional fees | 1,667 | 100 | 750 | 1,000 | 1,000 | 150 | 150 | 150 | 150 | 83 | | | | 5,200 |
| Contingency | | 230 | 230 | 230 | 230 | 230 | 230 | 230 | 230 | 230 | 230 | | | 2,300 |
| Cost monitoring fees | | 24 | 15 | 15 | 15 | 15 | 15 | 15 | 15 | 15 | 24 | | | 168 |

| | | | | | | | | | | | | | | Total |
|---|---|---|---|---|---|---|---|---|---|---|---|---|---|---|
| Legal/bank fees | | 830 | | | | | | | | | | | | 830 |
| Feasibility study | 80 | 64 | | | | | | | | | | | | 144 |
| Total cost excl. interest | 4,999 | 5,732 | 5,395 | 7,145 | 7,222 | 3,183 | 2,795 | 1,855 | 1,147 | 483 | 1,228 | | | 41,184 |
| Equity | 5,000 | 5,732 | 2,431 | | | | | | | | | | | 13,163 |
| Amount financed | | | 2,964 | 7,145 | 7,222 | 3,183 | 2,795 | 1,855 | 1,147 | 483 | 1,228 | | | 28,022 |
| Interest | | | | 27 | 92 | 159 | 190 | 217 | 236 | 249 | 256 | 270 | 272 | 1,968 |
| Loan balance | | | 2,964 | 10,136 | 17,450 | 20,792 | 23,777 | 25,849 | 27,232 | 27,964 | 29,448 | 29,718 | 29,990 | 29,990 |
| Total project cost excl. interest | 5,000 | 10,732 | 16,127 | 23,272 | 30,494 | 33,677 | 36,472 | 38,327 | 39,474 | 39,957 | 41,185 | 41,185 | 41,185 | 41,185 |
| Total project cost incl. interest | 5,000 | 10,732 | 16,127 | 23,299 | 30,586 | 33,836 | 36,662 | 38,544 | 39,710 | 40,206 | 41,441 | 41,455 | 41,457 | 43,153 |

**Table 7.5** ABC Hotel: Financial base (note: all figures in 000s).

| Assumptions | 1996 | 1997 | 1998 | 1999 | 2000 | 2001 | 2002 |
|---|---|---|---|---|---|---|---|
| No. of rooms | 253 | 253 | 253 | 253 | 253 | 253 | 253 |
| Occupancy rate | 55% | 61% | 58% | 62% | 68% | 68% | 68% |
| Rate per room/day | 195 | 225 | 245 | 270 | 284 | 298 | 313 |
| Days per year | 365 | 365 | 365 | 365 | 365 | 365 | 365 |

| Income statement projection | 1996 | 1997 | 1998 | 1999 | 2000 | 2001 | 2002 |
|---|---|---|---|---|---|---|---|
| **Operating revenues** | | | | | | | |
| Rooms | 9,904 | 12,674 | 13,122 | 15,459 | 17,834 | 18,713 | 19,627 |
| Food | 6,347 | 7,393 | 7,381 | 8,284 | 9,540 | 10,045 | 10,518 |
| Beverage | 0 | 0 | 0 | 0 | 0 | 0 | 0 |
| Food and beverage (other) | 0 | 0 | 0 | 0 | 0 | 0 | 0 |
| Telephone | 558 | 650 | 649 | 729 | 839 | 883 | 925 |
| Other operating dept | 558 | 650 | 649 | 729 | 839 | 883 | 925 |
| Commercial rentals | 0 | 0 | 0 | 0 | 0 | 0 | 0 |
| Health and leisure | 0 | 0 | 0 | 0 | 0 | 0 | 0 |
| Other income | 198 | 253 | 262 | 309 | 356 | 374 | 392 |
| **Total revenues** | **17,565** | **21,620** | **22,063** | **25,510** | **29,408** | **30,898** | **32,387** |

**Operating expenses**

| | | | | | | | |
|---|---|---|---|---|---|---|---|
| Rooms | 2,178 | 2,408 | 2,362 | 2,782 | 3,204 | 3,373 | 3,532 |
| Food and beverage | 5,078 | 5,692 | 5,535 | 6,213 | 7,155 | 7,534 | 7,889 |
| Telephone | 530 | 598 | 584 | 656 | 755 | 795 | 833 |
| Other operating dept | 419 | 487 | 487 | 510 | 587 | 618 | 647 |
| Commercial rentals | 0 | 0 | 0 | 0 | 0 | 0 | 0 |
| Health and leisure | 0 | 0 | 0 | 0 | 0 | 0 | 0 |
| Other income | 0 | 0 | 0 | 0 | 0 | 0 | 0 |
| **Total operating expenses** | **8,205** | **9,185** | **8,968** | **10,161** | **11,701** | **12,320** | **12,901** |
| | *47%* | *42%* | *41%* | *40%* | *40%* | *40%* | *40%* |

**Dept. operating income**

| | | | | | | | |
|---|---|---|---|---|---|---|---|
| Rooms | 7,726 | 10,266 | 10,760 | 12,677 | 14,630 | 15,340 | 16,095 |
| Food and beverage | 1,269 | 1,701 | 1,846 | 2,071 | 2,385 | 2,511 | 2,629 |
| Telephone | 28 | 52 | 65 | 73 | 84 | 88 | 92 |
| Other operating dept | 139 | 163 | 162 | 219 | 252 | 265 | 278 |
| Commercial rentals | 0 | 0 | 0 | 0 | 0 | 0 | 0 |
| Health and leisure | 0 | 0 | 0 | 0 | 0 | 0 | 0 |
| Other income | 198 | 253 | 262 | 309 | 356 | 374 | 392 |
| **Gross operating income** | **9,360** | **12,435** | **13,095** | **15,349** | **17,707** | **18,578** | **19,486** |
| *Contribution margin* | *53%* | *58%* | *59%* | *60%* | *60%* | *60%* | *60%* |

(continued overleaf)

**Table 7.5** (*Continued*).

| Assumptions | 1996 | 1997 | 1998 | 1999 | 2000 | 2001 | 2002 |
|---|---|---|---|---|---|---|---|
| **Deductions from income** | | | | | | | |
| Admin. and general | 1,493 | 1,794 | 1,765 | 2,040 | 2,350 | 2,474 | 2,591 |
| Marketing | 878 | 864 | 772 | 892 | 1,028 | 1,082 | 1,133 |
| Property operations | 439 | 713 | 882 | 1,020 | 1,175 | 1,237 | 1,295 |
| Energy | 966 | 1,124 | 1,103 | 1,275 | 1,468 | 1,546 | 1,619 |
| Other | 0 | 0 | 0 | 0 | 0 | 0 | 0 |
| **Total deductions from income** | **3,776** | **4,495** | **4,522** | **5,227** | **6,021** | **6,339** | **6,638** |
| Income before fixed charges | 5,584 | 7,940 | 8,573 | 10,122 | 11,686 | 12,239 | 12,848 |
| **Fixed charges** | | | | | | | |
| Management fees | 527 | 649 | 661 | 765 | 881 | 927 | 971 |
| Incentive management fee | 505 | 728 | 791 | 935 | 1,077 | 1,134 | 1,187 |
| Franchise fee | 0 | 0 | 0 | 0 | 0 | 0 | 0 |
| Fixtures, fittings, and equipment reserve | 175 | 432 | 661 | 765 | 881 | 927 | 971 |
| Leasehold rent | 9 | 9 | 10 | 10 | 11 | 11 | 12 |
| Insurance | 0 | 0 | 0 | 0 | 0 | 0 | 0 |
| Rates/property tax | 87 | 108 | 110 | 127 | 146 | 154 | 161 |
| Other | 0 | 0 | 0 | 0 | 0 | 0 | 0 |
| Total Fixed charges | 1,303 | 1,926 | 2,233 | 2,602 | 2,996 | 3,153 | 3,302 |
| *Net operating income (EBIT)* | *4,281* | *6,014* | *6,340* | *7,520* | *8,690* | *9,086* | *9,546* |

|  |  | 1996 | 1997 | 1998 | 1999 | 2000 | 2001 | 2002 |
|---|---|---|---|---|---|---|---|---|
| Interest expense |  | 3,300 | 3,300 | 3,271 | 3,238 | 3,128 | 2,941 | 2,721 |
| EBT |  | 981 | 2,714 | 3,069 | 4,281 | 5,561 | 6,144 | 6,825 |
| Taxes | 15% | 147 | 407 | 460 | 642 | 834 | 922 | 1,024 |
| Net income |  | 834 | 2,307 | 2,609 | 3,639 | 4,727 | 5,223 | 5,801 |

| Ratios | 1996 | 1997 | 1998 | 1999 | 2000 | 2001 | 2002 |
|---|---|---|---|---|---|---|---|
| EBITDA/interest | 1.30 | 1.82 | 1.94 | 2.32 | 2.78 | 3.09 | 3.51 |
| EBITDA/interest + capital | 1.30 | 1.69 | 1.78 | 1.77 | 1.80 | 1.84 | 1.92 |

| Debt service | 1996 | 1997 | 1998 | 1999 | 2000 | 2001 | 2002 |
|---|---|---|---|---|---|---|---|
| Loan | 11.0% | 11.0% | 11.0% | 11.0% | 11.0% | 11.0% | 11.0% |
|  | 30,000 | 30,000 | 29,740 | 29,440 | 28,440 | 26,740 | 24,740 |
| Interest | 3,300 | 3,300 | 3,271 | 3,238 | 3,128 | 2,941 | 2,721 |
| Principal repayment | 0 | 260 | 300 | 1,000 | 1,700 | 2,000 | 2,240 |
| Total debt service | 3,300 | 3,560 | 3,571 | 4,238 | 4,828 | 4,941 | 4,961 |

room rates, then you can quickly run alternative scenarios in terms of the operational cash flows. Table 7.6 shows a worst-case scenario. Starting at the input assumptions we have reduced occupation levels and also reduced room rates – a double blow to the business at the same time. Looking down the data, you can see the reduction in revenues and finally the collapse of the cash flow coverage ratios.

Whether the lenders will provide the term loan is another issue beyond our scope here. Our job was to provide cash flow data. The model is not complete but I am sure you get the idea! We can take it further to include more scenarios; we could also discount the future cash flows to assist with the project evaluation in terms of the cash flow returns on investment.

## CASE STUDY 3: AG BARR PLC AND JN NICHOLS (VIMTO) PLC

### Strategic cash flow management: Comparing cash flows

A very useful exercise for any corporate manager is to compare cash flows with another corporate operating in the same sector. For the purposes of illustration, I have chosen two publicly quoted companies of senior ranking, AG Barr plc and JN Nichols (Vimto) plc, both of whom manufacture soft drinks and have head offices domiciled within the UK. By way of example, I am presenting the 2001 performance of AG Barr (Tables 7.7 and 7.8) and the 2000 figures of JN Nichols (Vimto) (Tables 7.9 and 7.10).

AG Barr is known as the manufacturer of several soft drinks, the most famous of which is Irn Bru, which actually outsells Coca-Cola in Scotland! JN Nichols (Vimto) is predominantly known as the manufacturer of the soft drink Vimto. Both companies will, therefore, need to be careful in terms of cash management within the production process, plus cash will be needed for brand promotion and continuous capital investment in plant and machinery.

Reviewing the cash flows, both companies show tight working capital management, with net cash from operations positive at £10.27mn (Vimto) and £16.9mn (Barr). JN Nichols (Vimto) is cash-negative at £5.1mn after finance, taxation, dividends, and capex of

**Table 7.6**  ABC Hotel: Worst-case scenario (note: all figures in 000s).

| Assumptions | 1996 | 1997 | 1998 | 1999 | 2000 | 2001 | 2002 |
|---|---|---|---|---|---|---|---|
| No. of rooms | 253 | 253 | 253 | 253 | 253 | 253 | 253 |
| Occupancy rate | 55% | 60% | 60% | 60% | 60% | 60% | 60% |
| Rate per room/day | 150 | 150 | 150 | 150 | 150 | 150 | 150 |
| Days per year | 365 | 365 | 365 | 365 | 365 | 365 | 365 |

| Income statement projection | 1996 | 1997 | 1998 | 1999 | 2000 | 2001 | 2002 |
|---|---|---|---|---|---|---|---|
| **Operating revenues** | | | | | | | |
| Rooms | 7,618 | 8,311 | 8,311 | 8,311 | 8,311 | 8,311 | 8,311 |
| Food | 6,347 | 7,393 | 7,381 | 8,284 | 9,540 | 10,045 | 10,518 |
| Beverage | 0 | 0 | 0 | 0 | 0 | 0 | 0 |
| Food and beverage (other) | 0 | 0 | 0 | 0 | 0 | 0 | 0 |
| Telephone | 558 | 650 | 649 | 729 | 839 | 883 | 925 |
| Other operating dept | 558 | 650 | 649 | 729 | 839 | 883 | 925 |
| Commercial rentals | 0 | 0 | 0 | 0 | 0 | 0 | 0 |
| Health and leisure | 0 | 0 | 0 | 0 | 0 | 0 | 0 |
| Other income | 198 | 253 | 262 | 309 | 356 | 374 | 392 |
| **Total revenues** | 15,279 | 17,257 | 17,252 | 18,362 | 19,885 | 20,496 | 21,071 |
| Operating expenses | 47% | 42% | 41% | 40% | 40% | 40% | 40% |
| **Total operating expenses** | 7,137 | 7,331 | 7,012 | 7,314 | 7,912 | 8,172 | 8,393 |

(continued overleaf)

**Table 7.6**  (Continued).

| Assumptions | 1996 | 1997 | 1998 | 1999 | 2000 | 2001 | 2002 |
|---|---|---|---|---|---|---|---|
| **Dept operating income** | | | | | | | |
| **Gross operating income** | **8,142** | **9,926** | **10,240** | **11,048** | **11,973** | **12,324** | **12,678** |
| *Contribution margin* | *53%* | *58%* | *59%* | *60%* | *60%* | *60%* | *60%* |
| **Deductions from income** | | | | | | | |
| Admin. and general | 1,493 | 1,794 | 1,765 | 2,040 | 2,350 | 2,474 | 2,591 |
| Marketing | 878 | 864 | 772 | 892 | 1,028 | 1,082 | 1,133 |
| Property operations | 439 | 713 | 882 | 1,020 | 1,175 | 1,237 | 1,295 |
| Energy | 966 | 1,124 | 1,103 | 1,275 | 1,468 | 1,546 | 1,619 |
| Other | 0 | 0 | 0 | 0 | 0 | 0 | 0 |
| **Total deductions from income** | **3,776** | **4,495** | **4,522** | **5,227** | **6,021** | **6,339** | **6,638** |
| **Income before fixed charges** | **4,366** | **5,431** | **5,718** | **5,821** | **5,952** | **5,985** | **6,040** |
| **Fixed charges** | | | | | | | |
| Management fees | 527 | 649 | 661 | 765 | 881 | 927 | 971 |
| Incentive management fee | 505 | 728 | 791 | 935 | 1,077 | 1,134 | 1,187 |
| Franchise fee | 0 | 0 | 0 | 0 | 0 | 0 | 0 |
| Fixtures, fittings, and equipment reserve | 175 | 432 | 661 | 765 | 881 | 927 | 971 |
| Leasehold rent | 9 | 9 | 10 | 10 | 11 | 11 | 12 |
| Insurance | 0 | 0 | 0 | 0 | 0 | 0 | 0 |
| Rates/property tax | 87 | 108 | 110 | 127 | 146 | 154 | 161 |
| Other | 0 | 0 | 0 | 0 | 0 | 0 | 0 |
| **Total fixed charges** | **1,303** | **1,926** | **2,233** | **2,602** | **2,996** | **3,153** | **3,302** |

| | 1996 | 1997 | 1998 | 1999 | 2000 | 2001 | 2002 |
|---|---|---|---|---|---|---|---|
| *Net operating income* | 3,063 | 3,505 | 3,485 | 3,219 | 2,956 | 2,832 | 2,738 |
| Interest expense | 3,300 | 3,300 | 3,271 | 3,238 | 3,128 | 2,941 | 2,721 |
| **EBT** | **−237** | **205** | **213** | **−19** | **−172** | **−110** | **16** |
| Taxes  15% | 0 | 31 | 32 | 0 | 0 | 0 | 2 |
| **Net income** | **−237** | **174** | **181** | **−19** | **−172** | **−110** | **14** |

| Ratios | 1996 | 1997 | 1998 | 1999 | 2000 | 2001 | 2002 |
|---|---|---|---|---|---|---|---|
| EBITDA/interest | 0.93 | 1.06 | 1.07 | 0.99 | 0.94 | 0.96 | 1.01 |
| EBITDA/interest + capital | 0.93 | 0.98 | 0.98 | 0.76 | 0.61 | 0.57 | 0.55 |

| Debt service | 1996 | 1997 | 1998 | 1999 | 2000 | 2001 | 2002 |
|---|---|---|---|---|---|---|---|
| | 11.0% | 11.0% | 11.0% | 11.0% | 11.0% | 11.0% | 11.0% |
| Loan | 30,000 | 30,000 | 29,740 | 29,440 | 28,440 | 26,740 | 24,740 |
| Interest | 3,300 | 3,300 | 3,271 | 3,238 | 3,128 | 2,941 | 2,721 |
| *Principal repayment* | 0 | 260 | 300 | 1,000 | 1,700 | 2,000 | 2,240 |
| **Total debt service** | **3,300** | **3,560** | **3,571** | **4,238** | **4,828** | **4,941** | **4,961** |

**Table 7.7**  AG Barr plc: Cash flow statement for the year ended 2001.

|  | £'000 | £'000 |
|---|---|---|
| **Net cash inflow from operating activities** |  | 16932 |
| **Returns on investments and servicing of finance** |  |  |
| Interest received | 311 |  |
| Interest paid | (9) |  |
| Interest element of hire purchase paid | (77) |  |
| **Net cash outflow from returns on investments and servicing of finance** |  | 225 |
| **Taxation** |  |  |
| Corporation tax paid |  | (3821) |
| **Capital expenditure and financial investment** |  |  |
| Purchase of tangible fixed assets | (7115) |  |
| Grants received |  |  |
| Sale of tangible fixed assets | 188 |  |
|  |  | (6927) |
|  |  | (6409) |
| **Acquisitions and disposals** |  |  |
| Investment in associated undertaking |  |  |
| **Dividends paid** |  | (3811) |
| **Net cash flow before financing** |  | **(2598)** |

**Table 7.8**  AG Barr plc: Net cash inflow from operating activities for the year ended 2001.

|  | £'000 |
|---|---|
| Operating profit | 13697 |
| Depreciation | 5710 |
| (Gain) on sale of tangible fixed assets | 91 |
| Government grants written back | (52) |
| Decrease/(increase) in stocks | (1773) |
| (Increase)/decrease in debtors | (2670) |
| (Increase)/decrease in investment |  |
| Increase/(decrease) in creditors | 2193 |
| Pension provision release | 7 |
|  | 16932 |

**Table 7.9** JN Nicols (Vimto) plc: Consolidated cash flow statement for the year ended December 31, 2000.

| | £'000 | £'000 |
|---|---|---|
| **Cash inflow from operating activities** | | 10268 |
| **Returns on investments and servicing of finance** | | |
| Investment income | 18 | |
| Interest payable | (984) | |
| Interest element of hire purchase contracts | (8) | |
| **Net cash inflow from returns on investments and servicing of finance** | | (966) |
| **Taxation** | | (1995) |
| **Capital expenditure and financial investment** | | |
| Purchase of tangible fixed assets | (7463) | |
| Investment in own shares | – | |
| Proceeds of sales of tangible fixed assets | 297 | |
| **Net cash outflow for capital expenditure and financial investment** | | (7166) |
| **Acquisitions and disposals** | | |
| Purchase of subsidiary undertaking | (2130) | |
| Proceeds on part sale of subsidiary undertaking | 109 | |
| **Net cash inflow from acquisitions and disposals** | | (2021) |
| **Equity dividends paid** | | (3179) |
| **Net cash flow before financing** | | (5059) |

**Table 7.10** JN Nichols (Vimto) plc: Reconciliation of operating profit to net cash inflow from operating activities for the year ended December 31, 2000.

| | £'000 |
|---|---|
| Operating profit | 8525 |
| Depreciation | 4588 |
| Amortization of intangible fixed assets | 376 |
| Profit on sale of tangible fixed assets | (39) |
| Write-down of own shares | 103 |
| Increase in stocks | (1225) |
| Increase in debtors | (3238) |
| Increase in creditors | 1178 |
| | 10268 |

£7.5mn. AG Barr is cash-positive at £2.6mn even after high capex at £7.1mn relating to new factory production facilities.

## STRATEGIC CASH FLOW MANAGEMENT AND CAPITAL INVESTMENT

So far we have examined cash flow generated from operations and then the absorption or generation of cash within the working investment. Next we will look at the important area of capital expenditure and in particular how we can evaluate the proposed investment.

### Capital expenditure: Introduction to methods of appraisal

There are four main methods of capital investment appraisal. They have in common a concern with cash flows. They all, therefore, require an evaluation of the initial cost, the running expenses, the estimated life of the project, and the income over the life of the project. Only cash items are included in the calculation of these factors. This means that depreciation is ignored, but the expected residual value of the item in the marketplace is included. Taxation, which may be a cash inflow or outflow, can have a significant effect on an investment decision and should always be included.

The four methods are payback, average rate of return, net present value, and yield or internal rate of return.

### Method 1: Payback

This method calculates the time for cash inflows to recoup the initial investment on the project. The payback period indicates to management the time that the investment is at risk: the shorter the length of the period to payback, the better. This method is widely used because it is simple to understand. It provides a clear indication of the time required to convert a "risky" investment into a safe one Table 7.11. It does not, however, pay any heed to several factors, such as the timing of cash flows, the situation after the payback period, and the return on capital invested relative to the time value of money.

**Table 7.11** Capital expenditure decisions: Payback period (note: all figures in 000s). (Source: Pitcher, M.A. (1979) *Management Accounting for the Lending Banker*. The Institute of Bankers, London.).

| Cash price and all other initial costs | Machine A 50.0 | Machine B 50.0 | Machine C 70.0 |
|---|---|---|---|
| Net cash inflows | | | |
| Year 1 | 5.0 | 15.0 | 10.0 |
| Year 2 | 10.0 | 25.0 | 10.0 |
| Year 3 | 15.0 | 15.0 | 20.0 |
| Year 4 | 20.0 | 5.0 | 20.0 |
| Year 5 | 20.0 | 5.0 | 30.0 |
| Year 6 | 15.0 | 0 | 20.0 |
| Year 7 | 0 | 0 | 10.0 |
| Residual value (at end of last operating year | 1.0 | 0 | 2.0 |
| | 86.0 | 65.0 | 122.0 |
| Payback (years) | 4 | $2\frac{2}{3}$ | $4\frac{2}{3}$ |

## Method 2: Average rate of return

This method calculates the average annual net cash inflow as a percentage of the initial cash outflow. This may be represented by the formula:

Average annual net cash inflow/Initial cash outflow

This provides an entirely different kind of yardstick, which indicates the return earned on the capital employed. This method also has the advantage of simplicity, but continues to ignore the timing of cash flows (Table 7.12).

## Method 3: Net present value

Money can be said to have a time value - £1 today is worth more than £1 in a year's time, because it can be invested to earn interest. How much more it is worth will depend upon the rate of interest it can earn during the year. If it can be used to buy stocks or bonds paying 10%

**Table 7.12** Cash flow: Average rate of return on expenditure decisions (note: all figures in 000s). (Source: Pitcher, M.A. (1979) *Management Accounting for the Lending Banker*. The Institute of Bankers, London.).

| Cash price and all other initial costs | Machine A 50.0 | Machine B 50.0 | Machine C 70.0 |
|---|---|---|---|
| Net cash inflows – totals | 86.0 | 65.0 | 122.0 |
| Period of years | 6.0 | 5.0 | 7.0 |
| Average annual cash inflows | 14.3 | 13.0 | 17.4 |
| Average rate of return | 28.7% | 26.0% | 24.9% |

per annum, then it will be worth £1.10 in one year's time. Expressed another way, £1 received in one year's time is equivalent to 91p today (91p + 10% = £1.)

To arrive at a proper appraisal an allowance must be made for the timing of cash flows, and this is done by reducing the value of future incomings and outgoings to their present-day worth, using an appropriate rate of interest. This process is known as *discounting* and the factors may be calculated using the formula:

$$1/((1 + i)^n)$$

where $i$ is the rate of interest and $n$ the number of years. In practice, it is much easier to look up the figures in discounting tables.

To provide an additional assessment of the merits of each investment, the discounted inflows can be related to the original outlay to complete what is known as the *profitability index* (Table 7.13). The project with the highest profitability index is to be preferred.

## Method 4: Yield or internal rate of return

This is a refinement of the last method. It is used when managers wish to know the discount rate that exactly equates cash inflows with the outlay. This is sometimes to be preferred to assuming a rate.

The calculation is more time-consuming, as it involves using a trial-and-error method on at least two rates until the two figures are equal

**Table 7.13** Discounting cash flow method.

| | 10% discount | Machine A | | Machine B | | Machine C | |
|---|---|---|---|---|---|---|---|
| | | Actual value | Present value | Actual value | Present value | Actual value | Present value |
| Initial cash outflow | 1 | 50,000 | 50,000 | 50,000 | 50,000 | 70,000 | 70,000 |
| Net cash inflows (yr) | | | | | | | |
| 1 | 0.909 | 5,000 | 4,545 | 15,000 | 13,635 | 10,000 | 9,090 |
| 2 | 0.826 | 10,000 | 8,260 | 25,000 | 20,650 | 10,000 | 8,260 |
| 3 | 0.751 | 15,000 | 11,265 | 15,000 | 11,265 | 20,000 | 15,020 |
| 4 | 0.685 | 20,000 | 13,660 | 5,000 | 3,415 | 20,000 | 13,660 |
| 5 | 0.621 | 20,000 | 12,420 | 5,000 | 3,105 | 30,000 | 18,630 |
| 6 | 0.564 | 15,000 | 8,460 | | 0 | 20,000 | 11,280 |
| 7 | 0.513 | 0 | 0 | | 0 | 10,000 | 5,130 |
| Residual value | | 1,000 | 564 | | 0 | 2,000 | 1,026 |
| | | 86,000 | 59,174 | 65,000 | 52,070 | 122,000 | 82,096 |

(Table 7.14). This rate can then be compared with, say, the rate of any borrowed money, which may be required to finance the project, or the company's average cost of capital.

## Shortcomings of appraisal methods

One shortcoming is immediately obvious: not all methods give the same answer. The final choice must be made in the light of all the circumstances. It is a matter for managerial judgement as to whether the security of a short payback outweighs the disadvantage of lower profitability.

The forecasting of cash flows can also pose serious problems. Because of the longer-term nature of most capital investment, it is often extremely difficult to project timings and amounts for cash inflows and outflows, particularly during the later stages of the project. This can easily render any appraisal meaningless. Delays in installation of even comparatively simple machinery can quickly cause large variances from the plan, and escalating costs can rapidly eat up margins. In

**Table 7.14** Internal rate of return/DCF yield.

| | 14% discount | Machine A | | 16% discount | Present value |
|---|---|---|---|---|---|
| | | Actual value | Present value | | |
| Initial cash outflow | | 50,000 | 50,000 | | 50,000 |
| Net cash inflows (yr) | | | | | |
| 1 | 0.877 | 5,000 | 4,385 | 0.862 | 4,310 |
| 2 | 0.769 | 10,000 | 7,690 | 0.743 | 7,430 |
| 3 | 0.675 | 15,000 | 10,125 | 0.641 | 9,615 |
| 4 | 0.592 | 20,000 | 11,840 | 0.552 | 11,040 |
| 5 | 0.519 | 20,000 | 10,380 | 0.476 | 9,520 |
| 6 | 0.456 | 15,000 | 6,840 | 0.410 | 6,150 |
| Residual value | | 1,000 | 456 | 0.410 | 410 |
| | | 86,000 | 51,716 | | 48,475 |

many cases, some proportion of the net cash inflows is represented by expected cost savings, and these are often much more difficult to realize in practice than they are on paper. The machine, which was intended to dispense with the services of ten operatives and increase productivity by 30%, often looks much less economical after the first year of operation.

It is vital to take all cash items into account when completing the appraisal. It is easy to forget the cost of any additional working capital the project may require, particularly in the area of work in progress. Occasionally, new equipment can provide a reduction in the need for working capital and this should not be overlooked as a cash inflow or lower cash outflow.

## ADDITIONAL CASH FLOW MANAGEMENT

You will have seen how important it is to any business to fully analyze the cash tied up in differing parts of the capital cycle. For this reason it is suggested that the following additional analyses are made.

## Debtors

This figure needs breaking down into normal trade, intercompany, and doubtful debts. Care should be taken not to include any debts that have been factored under a factoring agreement. Further, it is useful to get an indication of debtor spread and debtor control. Tables 7.15 and 7.16 can be used in debtor analysis.

**Table 7.15**   Debtor analysis.

| Debtor | Totals | Age (days) | | | | Remarks |
|---|---|---|---|---|---|---|
| | | Current | 30 | 60 | 90 | |
| £1000 and over | | | | | | |
| Others | | | | | | |
| Percentages | 100% | % | % | % | % | |

**Table 7.16**   Debtor analysis by major customer account.

| Name | Total balance | Current | 30 days | 60 days | 90 days | Remarks |
|---|---|---|---|---|---|---|
| Totals | | | | | | |

## Stock

This figure is a difficult one for many businesses to provide. Frequently there will be many differing stock lines and the only accurate way is to carry out a physical stock-check. However, this difficulty can be overcome if the stock file is computerized. Often, though, in practice you will have to make an estimate based on stock movements during the month. A quarterly or even monthly physical stock-take should be encouraged to give a clear indicator of the actual stock position. A further complication is in businesses where there is ongoing product manufacture or job contracts: then it will be necessary to estimate work in progress.

Also stock can be invoiced from a supplier subject to reservation of title (Romalpa terms). This reservation means that goods supplied remain the property of the supplier until he is paid. Again this should be noted.

Table 7.17 can be used in stock analysis. It is useful, when stock is physically checked and valued, to mark the stock figure on the monitoring form accordingly.

**Table 7.17** Analysis of manufacturing stock.

| Month ended | | |
| --- | --- | --- |
| Stock | £ | as a % |
| Raw materials | | |
| Work in progress | | |
| Finished goods | | |
| Total stock* | | |
| *Reservation of title £ ... | | |

## Creditors

In addition to age analysis, it is also very useful to split the creditors' total into normal trade and preferential. In business we always need to keep a watch on the prioritization of our creditors. We should establish if there are any set-off trading positions between creditors and debtors, which might lead to counterclaims. Tables 7.18 and 7.19 can be used in creditor analysis.

**Table 7.18** Creditor analysis.

| | Totals | Age (days) | | | | Remarks |
| --- | --- | --- | --- | --- | --- | --- |
| Creditors £1000 and over | | Current | 30 | 60 | 90 | |
| Others | | | | | | |
| Percentages | 100% | % | % | % | % | |

**Table 7.19** Creditor analysis by major customer account.

|  | Totals | Age (days) |  |  |  | Remarks |
|---|---|---|---|---|---|---|
|  |  | Current | 30 | 60 | 90 |  |
| Creditor |  |  |  |  |  |  |
| Trade |  |  |  |  |  |  |
| Preferential creditors |  |  |  |  |  |  |
| VAT |  |  |  |  |  |  |
| PAYE/NIC etc. |  |  |  |  |  |  |
| Totals |  |  |  |  |  |  |

The management of these critical factors and their impact on the cash flow will be a key issue for strategic cash flow management, whether the business is large or small in terms of size and business sector.

# Key Concepts and Thinkers

This chapter aims to help with understanding the terminology of strategic cash flow management and encourages learning from the work of others. It covers:

» a glossary of terms; and
» selected books of four key thinkers.

## A GLOSSARY OF STRATEGIC CASH FLOW MANAGEMENT

**Accounting policies** – Those principles and practices applied by an entity that specify how the effects of transactions and other events are to be reflected in the accounts. For example, an entity may have a policy of revaluing fixed assets or of maintaining them at historical cost. Accounting policies do not include estimation techniques.

**Accounts payable** – American term for Creditors.

**Accounts receivable** – American term for Debtors.

**Accrual** – An expense, or a proportion thereof, not invoiced prior to the balance sheet date but included in the accounts, sometimes on an estimated basis.

**Accruals concept** – Income and expenses are recognized in the period in which they are earned or incurred, rather than the period in which they happen to be received or paid.

**Acquisition** – The purchase or takeover of one company by another. This can be financed by a mixture of cash and/or debt and the issue of shares in the acquiring company.

**Asset** – Any property or right owned by a company and having a monetary value. In UK accounting standards, assets are defined as "rights or other access to future economic benefits controlled by an entity as a result of past transactions or events."

**Balance sheet** – A statement describing what a business owns and owes at a particular date.

**Book value** – The value of an asset as it appears in the balance sheet.

**Break-even point** – The point at which business costs equate to revenues, so that the business makes no profit or loss.

**Capital budget** – A financial plan for investment projects.

**Capital employed** – The aggregate amount of long-term funds invested in, or lent to, the business and used by it in carrying out its operations.

**Cash conversion cycle** – The conversion of sales into cash.

**Cash flow forecast** – A statement of anticipated cash balances based on estimated cash inflows and outflows over a given period.

**Cash flow statement** – A statement of cash flows during the most recent accounting period. The required format for a cash flow statement is laid down by accounting standards.

**Comparability** – The requirement that, once an accounting policy for a particular item in the accounts has been adopted, the same policy should be used from one period to the next. Any change in policy must be fully disclosed. Comparability is also important when comparing entities in the same industry: these should be compared, wherever possible, using similar accounting policies.

**Contingent liability** – A possible obligation arising from past events whose existence will be confirmed only by the occurrence of one or more uncertain future events not wholly within the entity's control.

**Cost of good sold** – (or **cost of sales**) Those costs, usually raw materials, labour, and production overheads, directly attributable to goods that have been sold. The difference between sales and cost of goods sold is gross profit.

**Creditors** – Amounts due to those who have supplied goods or services to the business.

**Current asset** – An asset which, if not already in cash form, is expected to be converted into cash within 12 months of the balance sheet date.

**Current cost** – The convention by which assets are valued at the cost of replacement at the balance sheet date (net of depreciation for fixed assets).

**Current liability** – An amount owed which will have to be paid within 12 months of the balance sheet date.

**Current ratio** – The ratio of current assets to current liabilities in a balance sheet, providing a measure of business liquidity.

**Debentures** – Long-term loans, usually secured on the company's assets.

**Debtors** – Amounts due from customers to whom goods or services have been sold, but for which they have not yet paid.

**Deferred asset/liability** – An amount receivable or payable more than 12 months after the balance sheet date.

**Deferred taxation** – An estimate of a tax liability payable at some estimated future date, resulting from timing differences in the taxation and accounting treatment of certain items of income and expenditure.

**Depreciation** – An estimate of the proportion of the cost of a fixed asset which has been consumed during an accounting period, whether through use, obsolescence, or the passage of time.

**Discounted cash flow** – A method of determining current value by the discounting of future expected cash flows.

**Distribution** – The amount distributed to shareholders out of the profits of a company, usually in the form of a cash dividend.

**Dividend cover** – The ratio of the amount of profit reported for the year to the amount distributed.

**Dividend yield** – The ratio of the amount of dividend per share to the market share price of a listed company.

**Earnings per share** – The amount of profit (after tax and any extraordinary items) attributable to shareholders, divided by the number of ordinary shares in issue.

**EBIT** – Earnings (profit) before interest and tax.

**EBITDA** – Earnings (profit) before interest, tax, depreciation, and amortization. This measure of operating cash flow is considered to be an important measure of the performance of an entity.

**Estimation techniques** – The methods adopted by an entity to arrive at estimated monetary amounts for items in the accounts. For example, of the various methods that could be adopted for depreciation, the entity may select to depreciate using the straight-line method.

**Exceptional item** – Income or expenditure that, although arising from the ordinary course of business, is of such unusual size or incidence that it needs to be disclosed separately.

**Expense** – A cost incurred, or a proportion of a cost, the benefit of which is wholly used up in the earning of the revenue for a particular accounting period.

**Extraordinary item** – An item of material income or expenditure arising from outside the ordinary course of business. As a result of recent changes to accounting standards, it is considered that extraordinary items are extremely rare, if not non-existent.

**Fixed asset** – An asset held for use, rather than for sale, by a business.

**Fixed cost** – A cost that does not vary in proportion to changes in the scale of operations, e.g. rent.

**Free cash flow** – The amount of operating cash flow that is not required to fund the ongoing operations of a business.

**Gearing** – The word used to describe the financing of a company in terms of the proportion of capital provided by shareholders (equity) compared with the proportion provided by loan capital (debt).

**Gearing ratios** – There are many different ways to measure gearing. The commonest is probably the ratio of debt to equity, that is the ratio of interest-bearing liabilities to the net worth of a business. The income-gearing ratio is the ratio of interest payable to the profits out of which interest is paid, that is the ratio of interest to operating profit (EBIT or PBIT)

**Gross cash flow from operations** – The calculation is usually to take operating profits and add back non-cash items.

**Gross profit** – The difference between sales and the cost of goods sold.

**Historic cost convention** – The convention by which assets are valued on the basis of the original cost of acquiring or producing them.

**Interest cover** – The relationship between the amount of profit before interest and tax and the amount of interest payable during a period.

**Internal rate of return (IRR)** – The rate of return at which the net present value of an investment's cash flows equals zero.

**Leverage** – There are differing methods of calculation but the usual approach is to calculate the ratio of total liabilities to the net worth of a business.

**Liability** – An amount owed. In UK accounting standards, liabilities are defined as ''an entity's obligations to transfer economic benefits as a result of past transactions or events.''

**Liquidity** – A term used to describe the cash resources of a business and its ability to meet its short-term obligations.

**Listed investments** – Investments for which the market price is quoted on a recognized stock exchange. They may therefore be traded on that exchange.

**Long-term liability** – An amount payable more than 12 months after the balance sheet date.

**Market price** – The price of a quoted security for dealing in the open market.

**Net assets** – The amount of total assets less total liabilities.

**Net book value** – The cost or valuation of fixed assets less accumulated depreciation to date. Net book value bears no relationship to market value.

**Net current assets** – The amount of current assets less current liabilities.

**Net operating cash flow** – Cash flow generated from operations before financing obligations or discretionary uses.

**Net realizable value** – The amount for which an asset could be sold in its existing condition at the balance sheet date, after deducting any costs to be incurred in disposing of it.

**Nominal value** – The face value of a share or other security.

**Overhead** – Any expense, other than the direct cost of materials or labour, involved in making a company's products.

**PBIT** – (Earnings) profit before interest and tax.

**Prepayment** – The part of a cost which is carried forward as an asset in the balance sheet to be recognized as an expense in the ensuing period(s) in which the benefit will be derived from it, e.g. the payment in advance of rates.

**Price/earnings ratio** – The relationship between the market price of a share and its latest reported earnings per share.

**Profit** – The difference between the revenues earned in a period and the costs incurred in earning them. Alternative definitions are possible according to whether the figure is struck before or after tax.

**Profit and loss account** – A statement summarizing revenues, and the costs incurred in earning them, during an accounting period.

**Provision** – A liability of uncertain timing or amount. A provision should only be recognized in the balance sheet when an entity has a present obligation (legal or constructive) as a result of a past event. It is probable that a transfer of economic benefits will be required to settle the obligation, and a reliable estimate can be made of the amount of the obligation. Unless these conditions are met, no provision should be recognized.

**Quick ratio** – The ratio of those current assets readily convertible into cash (usually current assets less stock) to current liabilities.

**Revaluation reserve** – The increase in value of a fixed asset as a result of a revaluation. This needs to be included in the balance sheet as part of shareholders' funds in order to make the balance sheet balance.

**Revenue** – Money received from selling the product of a business.

**Revenue reserves** – The accumulated amount of profit less losses generated by a company since its incorporation and retained in it. Usually called Profit and loss account in the balance sheet.

**Share capital** – Stated in the balance sheet at its nominal value and, if fully paid and not subject to any share premium, representing the amount of money introduced into the company by its shareholders at the time the shares were issued.

**Shareholders' funds** – A measure of the shareholders' total interest in the company, represented by the total of share capital plus reserves.

**Share premium** – The surplus over and above nominal value received in consideration for the issue of shares.

**Straight-line method** – a method of depreciation in which the nominated asset in bookkeeping is depreciated in a series of equal amounts in regular instalments.

**Turnover** – Revenue from sales.

**Variable cost** – A cost that increases or decreases in line with changes in the level of activity.

**Working capital** – Current assets less current liabilities, representing the amount a business needs to invest (and which is continually circulating) in order to finance its stock, debtors, and work in progress.

**Work in progress** – Goods or services in the course of production or provision at the balance sheet date.

## KEY THINKERS

Based on my research, the list of key thinkers is extremely short when you consider the importance of business cash flows and how they affect each and every business small or large, public or private, whatever the sector and location.

Apart from Mr Micawber, whose famous words about cash flow management are quoted in Chapter 2, the first thinkers on the subject appear to be two associate professors at the University of Minnesota, James M. Gahlon and Robert L. Vigeland, who published an article entitled "Early warning signals using cash flow analysis" in 1988.[1] The article revolved around their analysis and thoughts based on a study of failed and non-failed American firms.

More recently, key thinkers have developed books on the subject, a selection of which are listed below.

## Alastair Graham

Alastair Graham is noted as the editor of *Cashflow Control*, a guide to the subject. In this book, he addresses the fundamentals of cash flow analysis; the development and implementation of control mechanisms; case studies in cash flow management; and exercises for enhancing cash flow control.

Graham is also known as the editor of *Cashflow Forecasting and Liquidity*, a guide to a related topic. The title includes planning and preparation for forecasting cash flow; the importance of liquidity in financial management; the establishment of baseline models; case studies in forecasting and liquidity; and sample exercises.

### Highlights

Books:

» (ed.) (2001) *Cashflow Control*. Fitzroy Dearborn, London.
» (ed.) (2001) *Cashflow Forecasting and Liquidity*. Fitzroy Dearborn, London.

## Murray Dropkin and Allyson Hayden

Murray Dropkin and Allyson Hayden are noted as the authors of *The Cash Flow Management Book for Non-Profits: A step by step guide for managers and boards*. In this guide, they show non-profit leaders how their organizations can use cash flow as a powerful strategic tool. The authors walk the reader through the nuts and bolts of cash flow management and offer guidance in how to identify the primary source of revenue.

### Highlights

Books:

» (2001) *The Cash Flow Management Book for Non-Profits: A step by step guide for managers and boards*. Jossey-Bass/Wiley, Chichester.

## Keith Checkley

The author of the present book is best known for his best-selling title *Cash is Still King*. In the title, he maintains that cash is the lifeblood of any business, arguing that nothing provides a clearer picture of the financial strength or weakness of a business than an understanding of its cash flow strategy. The book is divided into three parts.

1 Cash flow and business management.
2 Cash flow and banking relationships.
3 Cash flow and restructuring or reorganizing a business.

## Highlights

Books:

» (2001) *Cash is Still King*. Fitzroy Dearborn, Chicago, IL.

## NOTE

1 Gahlon, J.M. & Vigeland, R.L. (December 1988) "Early warning signs of bankruptcy using cash flow analysis." *Journal of Commercial Bank Lending*. Robert Morris Associates, Philadelphia, PA.

# Resources

This chapter highlights the many useful resources relating to strategic cash flow management. It covers:

» articles from financial periodicals, newspapers, etc.;
» business books; and
» company accounts.

## PRESS AND PERIODICALS

In trying to improve knowledge and keep up to date on strategic cash flow management, it is very important to read both press and periodicals. The *Financial Times* and the *Wall Street Journal* are available in almost every country of the world and contain a vast amount of financial information. You may also wish to consult the articles in the following list in order to gather more information on our topic.

### Article 1

**Title:** "Managing cash flow: Taking a strategic view."
**Author(s):** Sharma, R. & Jones, S.
**Source:** *Australian CPA*, Feb. 2000, vol. 70 no. 1, Australia.
**Start page:** 32.
**No. of pages:** 2.
**Content:** Restates the importance of managing cash flow, illustrates the cash flow cycle, and discusses five aspects of its improvement. Starts with the identification of the key elements of the cycle for the individual business, followed by better internal control and accountability and regular cash flow forecasts. Provides a flow chart for reviewing short-term finance and advises the use of feedback to achieve continuous improvement.
**Keyword(s):** Cash flow, cash control, cash management, forecasting, feedback.
**Classification(s):** Accounting and finance – cash control.
**Style:** Technical.

### Article 2

**Title:** "Accruals and the prediction of future cash flows."
**Author(s):** Barth, M.E., Cram, D.P., & Nelson K.K.
**Source:** *Accounting Review*, Jan. 2001, vol. 76 no. 1, US.
**Start page:** 27.
**No. of pages:** 32.
**Content:** Shows that it is easier to predict future cash flows by disaggregating accruals into major components, than to use several lags of aggregate earnings. Identifies specific significant components: first,

change in accounts receivable; second, change in accounts payable; third, change in inventory; fourth, depreciation; and fifth, amortization. Models the working capital accrual process, avoiding industry-specific differences in accounting policies and practices. Uses 10,164 firm-year observations for non-financial firms from 1987 to 1996, looking at earnings, cash from operations and accruals, regressing future cash flow or current and past aggregate earnings, and current cash flow and components of accruals. Notes that each component is significant and of the predicted sign, in particular depreciation of long-lived tangible assets and amortization of intangible assets. Establishes that the effects are much better than from disaggregating cash flow from aggregate accruals.

**Keyword(s):** Cash flow, forecasting, accounts management, US.
**Classification(s):** Accounting and finance – cash control.
**ISSN:** 0001–4826.

## Article 3

**Title:** "A comparables approach to measuring cash flow-at-risk for non-financial firms."
**Author(s):** Stein, J.C., Usher S.E., LaGattuta, D., & Youngen, J.
**Source:** *Journal of Applied Corporate Finance*, Winter 2001, vol. 13 no. 4, US.
**Start page:** 100.
**No. of pages:** 10.
**Content:** Defines a cash flow-at-risk (C-FaR) measure for horizons of up to a year in non-financial firms. Projects C-FaR for Coca-Cola, Dell, and Cygnus one year ahead, looking at the size of their tails in terms of earnings. Proposes C-FaR as a useful support to discounted cash flow measures. Suggests how C-FaR can help define capital structure policy, risk management policy, and managing investors' expectations abut earnings volatility. Builds a model based on operating cash flow and book assets, forecasting one quarter and one year ahead using data from 1994 to 1999. Analyzes forecast errors for 81 subsamples in order to identify patterns: smaller and riskier firms have more extreme tail values. Suggests modifications such as customized, centered peer group comparison; or single-industry analysis (e.g. the electricity industry). Concludes that C-FaR is accurate and non-parametric.

**Keyword(s):** Cash flow, capital structure, forecasting, US.
**Classification(s):** Accounting and finance – cash control.
**Style:** Theoretical with a worked example.
**ISSN:** 1078-1196.

## Article 4

**Title:** "How fast can your company afford to grow?"
**Author(s):** Churchill, N.C. & Mullins, J.W.
**Source:** *Harvard Business Review*, May 2001, vol. 79 no. 5, US.
**Start page:** 135.
**No. of pages:** 9.
**Content:** Emphasizes the importance of striking a balance between generating and consuming cash when starting or growing a business. Sets out a framework for managing growth to take into account the company's operating cash cycle, as well as the amount of cash brought in by and necessary to finance each dollar of sales. Provides a worked example in order to establish the maximum self-financing growth rate for a hypothetical company. Identifies three levers available to improve the growth rate that can be achieved without recourse to additional financing: speeding up cash flow, reducing costs, and increasing prices. Comments upon factors adding additional complexity, such as income taxes, depreciation, and asset replacement. Introduces the effects of investment in additional fixed assets, R & D, and marketing, and comments on the differing operating characteristics evident in different product lines or with different customers or business units. Reviewer comments: brings together operations and asset management in one framework.
**Keyword(s):** Growth, business development, cash flow, assets management.
**Classification(s):** Accounting and finance – growth; public sector management; rapid management intelligence.
**Style:** Technical.
**ISSN:** 0017-8012

## Article 5

**Title:** "Investment-cash flow sensitivities are not valid measures of financing constraints."

**Author(s):** Kaplan, S.N. & Zingales, L.
**Source:** *Quarterly Journal of Economics*, May 2000, vol. 115 no. 2, US.
**Start page:** 707.
**No. of pages:** 6.
   **Content:** Responds to Fazzari, Hubbard, and Petersen (2000) by rejecting their criticisms of Kaplan and Zingales (1997) (KZ) while asserting that their main arguments support KZ. Points out that the disagreement is over how pervasive non-monotonicity is in the degree of financing constraints for investment-cash flow sensitivities. Argues that there is no definition of sufficient conditions for monotonicity and defends KZ's classification as reducing the ambiguity of objective criteria by considering management statements of liquidity. Takes as an example Microsoft's high cash holdings but obvious lack of financial constraint, and considers sensitivities to be partially caused by excessive managerial conservatism.
**Keyword(s):** Cash flow, investment, financing, liquidity, financial distress, US.
**Classification(s):** Accounting and finance – financial investment; social economics.
**ISSN:** 0033-5533.

## Article 6

**Title:** "Short-term liquidity management."
**Author(s):** Emmins, N., Bullock, A., Nicholson, M., Henney, G., Harris-Jones, J., Christopher, M., Lovett, D., & Hodgkinson, R.
**Source:** *The Treasurer*, Jan. 2000, UK.
**Start page:** 25.
**No. of pages:** 17.
**Content:** Describes the options available for short-term liquidity management, comparing the cost of overnight and overdraft borrowing, and the contract between borrowing and deposit rates, as well as proposing alternative investment instruments such as commercial paper or certificates of deposit. Illustrates liquidity management techniques by Laporte's cash management patterns, where the treasury acts as an in-house bank. Suggests that UK money market funds may follow US patterns, reducing diversification and credit risk, increasing liquidity flexibility, and reducing costs in a simple and easy way. Looks

at short-term cash flow techniques, which have to be customized for each firm, and at the factors that make short-term liquidity important for venture capitalists. Recommends small firms open accounts with smaller banks, cheaper than the big four, and gives some recipes for corporate recovery.

**Keyword(s):** Treasury management, liquidity, cash management, banking, financial risk, Laporte, UK.

**Classification(s):** Accounting and finance – cash control; rapid management intelligence.

**Style:** Technical.

**ISSN:** 0264-0937.

## Article 7

**Title:** "Cash management."

**Author(s):** Nicholson, M., Johnson, W., Maisuria, R., Smith, A., Queree, A., & Duff, A.G.

**Source:** *The Treasurer*, Apr. 2001, UK.

**Start page:** 32.

**No. of pages:** 21.

**Content:** Surveys eight cash management banks, identifying their aim to improve reporting services using the Web, to exploit automated cross-border euro sweeps and automated investment, and to introduce notional pooling if the regulatory obstacles can be overcome. Explains the obstacles and how P&O overcame them. Describes Diageo's centralized euro liquidity management strategy and its pooling structure. Demonstrates Marconi's global cash flow forecasting network, Aon's short-term investment of its money market funds, and Laporte's global management system with multilateral netting through its relationship banks.

**Keyword(s):** Treasury management, cash management, euro, financial investment, Diageo, Laporte, Marconi, P&O, Aon.

**Classification(s):** Accounting and finance – Treasury; rapid management intelligence.

**ISSN:** 0264-0937.

## Article 8

**Title:** "Would you credit IT? (credit control)."

**Author(s):** Sweet, P.

**Source:** *Accountancy*, Feb. 2000, vol. 125 no. 1278, UK.
**Start page:** 39.
**No. of pages:** 3.
**Content:** Recognizes that failures of UK small- and medium-sized enterprises are usually caused by cash flow problems and considers how new computer software, online databases, and/or CD-ROMs can provide information to help avoid accepting poor payers as credit customers. Describes some of the products and services available for both customer choice and credit control procedures, including those resulting from e-commerce. Lists relevant Websites for further information.
**Keyword(s):** Credit control, cash flow, computer software, online computing, UK.
**Classification(s):** Accounting and finance – cash control; information management and technology – software applications.
**Style:** Technical/journalistic.
**ISSN:** 0001–4664.

## Article 9

**Title:** "Security alert."
**Source:** *Asiamoney*, Apr. 2000, vol. 11 no. 3.
**Start page:** 31.
**No. of pages:** 1.
**Content:** Focuses on the security aspects of e-commerce in Hong Kong, China. Impact of e-commerce on cash management; enhancement of cash management in terms of information flows, decision-making, operations, and system maintenance; examples of technologically driven cash management products.
**Keyword(s):** Electronic commerce – China/Hong Kong; cash management – China/Hong Kong.
**AN:** 3470211.
**ISSN:** 0958–9309.

## Article 10

**Title:** "CashWare provides a key solution for treasuries."
**Author(s):** A.Q.
**Source:** *Corporate Finance*, Oct. 1998, no. 167.

**Start page:** 17.
**No. of pages:** 2.
**Content:** Reports on CashWare's offering of an outsourced cash management service to companies wishing to gain greater control over their cash flows. Use of Internet technologies to build an extranet environment for secure communications between a company's treasury, group subsidiaries, and external trading partners; Functionality for a number of internal cash management processes.
**Keyword(s):** Cash management, software, CashWare.
**AN:** 1239780.
**ISSN:** 0958-2053.

## Article 11

**Title:** "Making cash flow."
**Author(s):** Morphy, E.
**Source:** *Export Today*, July 98, vol. 14 no. 7.
**Start page:** 22.
**No. of pages:** 6.
**Content:** Focuses on the challenges an average global company can encounter in cash management. Information on Unilever Co.'s financial system and the European financial infrastructure; information on the savings that can be gained from electronic commerce; reference to the Uniform Electronic Transactions Act.
**Keyword(s):** Cash management, electronic commerce.
**AN:** 975800.
**ISSN:** 0882-4711.

## Article 12

**Title:** "CEOs of fast-growing companies share experiences."
**Author(s):** Doucet, K.
**Source:** *CMA Management*, June 2000, vol. 74 no. 5.
**Start page:** 9.
**No. of pages:** 2.
**Content:** Lists the top challenges faced by chief executive officers (CEOs) of high-growth companies in Ontario. Account of the problems encountered in cash flow management; role of CEOs in choosing

partners and strategic alliances to ensure alignment; factors to be considered by CEOs in employee hiring.

**Keyword(s):** Chief executive officers, business enterprises, Ontario.

**AN:** 3465798.

**ISSN:** 1490–4225.

## Article 13

**Title:** "Valuing dot-coms after the fall."

**Author(s):** Koller, T.M.

**Source:** *McKinsey Quarterly*, 2001 special edition no. 2, US.

**Start page:** 103.

**No. of pages:** 4

**Content:** Provides an analysis of investors' valuations of Internet companies. Importance of cash flow in determining value; long-term discounted cash flow analysis of Internet companies; development of a perspective for analyzing companies with no profits and negative cash flows; revenue generation; structural characteristics for high returns of capital; relevant market size.

**Keyword(s):** Internet industry, investments, valuation, e-commerce.

**AN:** 4427015.

**ISSN:** 0047–5394.

## Article 14

**Title:** "Plugging in finance to complete the flow of e-commerce."

**Author(s):** Pyne, J.M.

**Source:** *Strategic Finance*, May 2000, vol. 81 no. 11, US.

**Start page:** 34

**No. of pages:** 4

**Content:** Looks at the role of finance in e-commerce, taking United Parcel Service as an example of a company that makes full use of its IT systems to improve supply chain management and customer service, and that has used its own cash flow to offer various financial services to customers. Considers how other companies could add financial products to their e-commerce, e.g. electronic bill presentation and payment that reduce costs for the biller and the payer. Predicts that 75% of bill payments will be made via the Internet by 2005 and outlines a scenario showing how to take advantage of this.

**Keyword(s):** Financial services, payments, e-commerce, US.
**Classification(s):** Accounting and finance – information; information management and technology – purchasing.
**Style:** Case study/technical.
**ISSN:** 1524–833X.

## Article 15

**Title:** "Recent developments in CTM systems."
**Author(s):** Large, J.
**Source:** *The Treasurer*, May 1999, UK.
**Start page:** 27.
**No. of pages:** 2.
**Content:** Reviews the developments during 1998 among cash and treasury management (CTM) systems. Focuses on the success of PeopleSoft and SAP as suppliers of ERP systems, and the concentration of supply in a small number of companies. Explains the differences between systems in Internet capability and report generation, and new developments in external links, cash flow analysis, and real-time pricing. Looks at value-added support services that competitors are offering, and at treasury business solutions, offering a full package over a period of years. Concludes that CTM is becoming central to company operations.
**Keyword(s):** Treasury management, cash management, outsourcing, computer software, UK.
**Classification(s):** Accounting and finance – Treasury; information management and technology; rapid management intelligence.
**Style:** Technical.
**ISSN:** 0264–0937.

## Article 16

**Title:** "Virtual-e-teams making e-business-sense."
**Author(s):** Barekat, M.M.
**Source:** *Manufacturing Engineer*, Apr. 2001, vol. 80 no. 2, UK.
**Start page:** 66.
**No. of pages:** 4.
**Content:** Investigates emerging e-commerce infrastructures, which offer small firms the opportunity to make use of the technology without heavy investment. Welcomes a number of consequences of the stock

exchange demise of the dot.com company in April 2000: the ending of the Internet hype; a redirection of e-entrepreneurs' ideology and business strategy towards collaboration for mutual gain; a new focus on applying e-technology to solve real transition challenges towards the Internet-worked economy; the belated arrival of XML technology; and the arrival of new technology application service providers offering secure virtual e-business infrastructures and management applications. Discusses the virtues of renting rather than buying e-business infrastructures, which would enable the adoption of best practice business processes and allow businesses to manage their costs and control their cash flow more precisely. Suggests that, today, businesses of every size can afford to utilize enhanced and integrated derivatives of virtual infrastructure technologies. Looks ahead to the arrival of a whole new set of business structures and e-business models, the emergence of virtual e-teams, and the virtual testing of strategic business undertakings.

**Keyword(s):** Electronic commerce, virtual reality, infrastructure, Internet, teams.

**Classification(s):** Operations and production management – information technology.

**Style:** Journalistic.

**ISSN:** 0956-9944.

## FURTHER READING

### Books and articles

Altman, E.I. (Sept. 1968) "Financial ratios, discriminant analysis and the prediction of corporate bankruptcy." *Journal of Finance,* vol. 23, no. 4, pp. 589–609.

Altman, E.I. (1971) *Corporate Bankruptcy in America.* D.C. Heath & Co., Lexington, MA.

Altman, E.I. (1984) "The success of business failure prediction models: An International Survey." *Journal of Banking and Finance*, no. 8, pp. 171–98.

Andrews (1971) "The formulation of business strategy," *Harvard Business Review.*

Ansoff, H.I. (1965) *Corporate Strategy: An analytic approach to Business Policy for Growth and Expansion.* Penguin, Harmondsworth.

Argenti, J. (1976) *Corporate Collapse: The causes and symptoms*. McGraw-Hill, London.

Bathory, A. (1987) *The Analysis of Credit: Foundations and development of corporate credit assessment*. McGraw-Hill, London.

Beaver, W.H. "Financial ratios as predictors of failure." *Journal of Accounting Research,* vol. 5, pp. 71-111.

Bibeault, D.M. (1981) *Corporate Turnaround: How managers turn losers into winners*. McGraw-Hill, New York.

Boyadjian, H.J. & Warren, J.F. (1987) *Risks: Reading corporate signals*. John Wiley & Sons, Chichester.

Buchele, R. (1962) "How to evaluate a firm." *California Management Review,* pp. 5-16.

Casey, D.H. (July/August 1992) "Cash flows from operations: Why it deserves more attention." *Corporate Controller Journal*, vol. 4 no. 6, pp. 46-8.

Enderlein, E. (c. 1989) "Credit analysis: The power of cash-flow analysis." *Commercial Lending Review.*

Gahlon, J.M. & Vigeland, R.L. (December 1988) "Early warning signs of bankruptcy using cash flow analysis." *Journal of Commercial Bank Lending.*

Hiltz, K.A. & Gail, K.M. (October 1991) "Settling corporate workouts." *Business Credit Journal,* vol. 93 no. 9, pp. 8-10.

Jury, T.H. (1989) "Understanding money in business." Unpublished article, FSMD, Cheshire.

Kotler, P. (1972) *Stages of the Life Cycle*. Prentice Hall.

KPMG (2000) *Global Accounting UK, IAS, and US Compared*. Available online at: www.kpmg.com/Rut2000_prod/Documents/7/GAAP.pdf

The Lex Column (April 21, 1992) "When cash flow is king." *Financial Times.*

Manchester Business School (1988) *Corporate Strategic Planning*. Manchester Business School.

McIntosh, W. (July 19, 2001) "NTL in crisis talks with France Telecom." *Independent.*

McKinsey & Co. (1979) *Economic Value to the Customer*. Forbus and Mehta.

Millward, D. (November 10, 2000) "Why Dome was doomed to fail." *Daily Telegraph.*

Norgard, R.S. (April 1987) "The causes of corporate collapse." *Australian Accountant (Australia) Journal*, vol. 57 no. 3, pp. 24-5.

O'Connell, J.B. (April 1990) "How inventory appraisals are done." *Journal of Commercial Bank Lending.*

Pitcher, M.A. (1979) *Management Accounting for the Lending Banker*. The Institute of Bankers, London.

Porter, M. (1980) *Competitive Strategy: Techniques for analyzing industries and Competitors*. New York Free Press.

Reilly, A.H. (Spring 1987) "Are organizations ready for a crisis? A managerial scorecard." *Columbia Journal of World Business*, vol. 22 no. 1, pp. 79-88.

Scherer, P.S. (c.1988) "The turnaround consultant steers corporate renewal." *Journal of Management Consulting.*

Schulman, E.M. (June 1988) "Two methods for a quick cash flow analysis." *Journal of Commercial Bank Lending.*

Slatter, S. (1984) *Corporate Recovery: Successful turnaround strategies and their implementation*. Penguin, Harmondsworth.

Smith, T. (1992) *Accounting for Growth: Stripping the camouflage from company accounts*. Century, London.

Stevens, M. (Nov/Dec 1988) "Turning around a troubled company." *D&B Reports Journal*, vol. 36 no. 6, pp. 50-51.

Tucker, S.A. (1980) *Profit Planning Decisions with the Break-even System*. Gower, Farnborough, Hants.

Werner, L.R. (1990) "When crisis strikes use a message action plan." *Public Relations Journal*, vol. 4 no. 8, pp. 30-31.

Whaller, D. & Urry, M. (Feb. 22, 1991) "Cashflow becomes the determining factor," *Financial Times.*

## Annual accounts

AG Barr plc 2001.

Dell Corporation Business Metrics 1996/1997.

JN Nichols (Vimto) 2000.

# Ten Steps to Making it Work

This chapter provides some key insights into developing a 10-step process. The 10 steps are.

1 Review the capital cycle.
2 List the key areas applicable to your business.
3 Use the Du Pont methodology to check out your asset efficiency position.
4 Extract a summary of your historic cash flows on an annualized basis, using the direct or indirect method of cash flow statements.
5 Download from Websites, or obtain competitor accounts, in order to conduct comparative analysis.
6 Look closely at your cash conversion cycle – how quickly are you turning sales into cash?
7 Prepare a cash flow worksheet, detailing monthly receipts and expenses.
8 Extend the worksheet into a monthly cash flow forecast and then prepare three-year annualized forecasts on cash flows using the template provided in Chapter 3.

9 Run some sensitivity analysis on the resulting cash flows to see what flexing can achieve an improved end cash flow position – is the business a cash generator or cash consumer?

10 Calculate cash flow generation ratios – can you finance any predicted cash shortfalls?

At this final stage, we need to pull together a summary of 10 steps to facilitate our strategic cash flow management. Further detail on all these steps can be found in the earlier narrative in Chapters 1 to 9. The principles lying behind this section are to:

» use this guide to review your own cash flow management techniques;
» make comparisons with similar businesses within your own industry sector;
» keep abreast of updated tools and techniques via the e-learning environment; and
» make improvements to your cash flow by keeping this topic foremost in the business planning process.

## STEPS

1 Review the capital cycle.
2 List the key areas applicable to your business.
3 Use the Du Pont methodology to check out your asset efficiency position.
4 Extract a summary of your historic cash flows on an annualized basis, using the direct or indirect method of cash flow statements.
5 Download from Websites, or obtain competitor accounts, in order to conduct comparative analysis.
6 Look closely at your cash conversion cycle – how quickly are you turning sales into cash?
7 Prepare a cash flow worksheet, detailing monthly receipts and expenses.
8 Extend the worksheet into a monthly cash flow forecast and then prepare three-year annualized forecasts on cash flows using the template provided in Chapter 3.
9 Run some sensitivity analysis on the resulting cash flows to see what flexing can achieve an improved end cash flow position – is the business a cash generator or cash consumer?
10 Calculate cash flow generation ratios – can you finance any predicted cash shortfalls?

## 1 AND 2. REVIEW THE CAPITAL CYCLE. LIST THE KEY AREAS APPLICABLE TO YOUR BUSINESS

In order to complete the analysis of the cash flow of a business, it is first necessary to develop a thorough grasp of the various components that make up the flow of cash through the business. Cash is continually needed to finance the asset conversion cycle, to enable payments to the bank, to pay dividends to shareholders, to pay taxes due, to purchase further fixed assets, and to undertake research and development.

Cash can be seen in Fig. 2.1 (see Chapter 2) as the central hub of the capital cycle. *Good strategic cash flow management will effectively manage all the items within the cash flow capital cycle.*

## 3. USE THE DU PONT METHODOLOGY TO CHECK OUT YOUR ASSET EFFICIENCY POSITION

In 1909, the American manufacturer Du Pont introduced a system of management control ratios for the monitoring and control of business performance, incorporating profitability ratios and the utilization of cash flow, within the context of asset investment and return. Since that time, ratio and cash flow analysis has developed into many sophisticated formats. However it is worth restating Du Pont's original formula (Equation 10.1).

Return on assets (ROA) = (Income/Sales)

$$\times \text{ (Sales)/(Total assets)} \qquad (10.1)$$

The left side of the formula focuses on profitability ratios and the right side looks at asset utilization. By monitoring performance of the key ratio, ROA, a corporate can check annual trends of return on assets and then compare its performance with corporates in similar industrial sectors. The second use is the ability to carry out a diagnostic check. By analyzing profitability ratios we can check on trading margins, and by analyzing asset utilization ratios we can check on the effective utilization of assets and the resultant effect on cash flow movements. The return on assets can be seen to be, therefore, a multiple of the profit margin on sales and the rate of asset turnover. If the overall return is improving, it must be due to improved profitability or improved asset usage, or both!

## 4. EXTRACT A SUMMARY OF YOUR HISTORIC CASH FLOWS ON AN ANNUALIZED BASIS, USING THE DIRECT OR INDIRECT METHOD OF CASH FLOW STATEMENTS

In November 1987, the Financial Accounting Standards Board (FASB) adopted Statement of Financial Accounting Standards No. 95 – Statement of Cash Flows – which requires the inclusion of a statement of cash flows whenever a full set of financial statements is prepared. The FASB pronouncement permits one of two methods – direct or indirect – for calculating cash flows. Under the direct method, the actual cash inflows and outflows associated with operating activities are presented. The new accounting rules encourage this method of presentation but also permit an indirect method of calculation that starts with net income and makes a series of adjustments for depreciation, deferred taxes, gains and losses on sales of equipment and businesses, and changes in working capital.

### The direct method

A direct method for calculating cash flows, the uniform credit analysis (UCA) cash flow statement is highly structured and reveals the actual cash inflow or outflow of each item on the income statement. Its calculation of cash net income begins with cash receipts from sales and then makes deductions for suppliers, employees, creditors, and stockholders, as well as the government in the form of taxes. With its focus on actual cash flows and its specific identification of such items as cash flow from sales activity, cash cost of goods sold, and mandatory debt retirement, it yields additional information on the structure of cash flows that cannot be found in an indirect approach. Also, its standardized format facilitates comparisons across firms.

## 5. DOWNLOAD FROM WEBSITES, OR OBTAIN COMPETITOR ACCOUNTS, IN ORDER TO CONDUCT COMPARATIVE ANALYSIS

By way of example, I am presenting the 2001 performance of AG Barr and the 2000 figures of JN Nichols (Vimto) (see Tables 7.7, 7.8, 7.9, and 7.10 in Chapter 7). AG Barr is known as the manufacturer of several soft drinks, the most famous of which is Irn Bru, which actually outsells Coca-Cola in Scotland! JN Nichols (Vimto) is predominantly known as the manufacturer of the soft drink Vimto. Both companies will, therefore, need to be careful in terms of cash management within the production process, plus cash will be needed for brand promotion and continuous capital investment in plant and machinery.

Reviewing the cash flows, both companies show tight working capital management, with net cash from operations positive at £10.27mn (Vimto) and £16.9mn (Barr). JN Nichols (Vimto) is cash-negative at £5.1mn after finance, taxation, dividends, and capex of £7.5mn. AG Barr is cash-positive at £2.6mn even after high capex at £7.1mn relating to new factory production facilities.

## 6. LOOK CLOSELY AT YOUR CASH CONVERSION CYCLE – HOW QUICKLY ARE YOU TURNING SALES INTO CASH?

For the purposes of illustration, let's cross the Atlantic and pick up Dell Corporation of the US. The business was achieving growth but how could this be best managed in terms of cash flow? Russ Banham reported in the December 1997 *CFO Magazine* for senior executives that Dell's cash flow was the subject of close involvement by the corporate treasurer and the CFO. Readers will see some dramatic results:

"In the here-today, gone-tomorrow business of computers, speed saves. Nobody knows that better than Tom Meredith of Dell Computer Corp. Since taking the CFO position at the Round Rock, Texas based company in 1993 – a job the former treasurer of Sun Micosystems Inc. nearly rejected because of the monumental challenge – Meredith has made velocity his mantra, and liquidity improvement his personal crusade. 'I've always been grounded in the belief, right or wrong, that a company's focus on cash flow has nothing but a good impact on its operating performance," he says.

Dell's finance re-engineering effort was born of necessity in late 1995. The company's inventories were ballooning, accounts receivables were rising faster than its revenue growth rates, and asset management was undermined by several quarters of lackluster performance. Meredith notes "We needed to take the weight off the growth pedal and shift our focus to liquidity and profitability."

## Turning sales into cash

"We sent out a consistent message to everyone to focus on three things – asset management, return on invested capital, and cash conversion." Speed is of the essence. "Basically, we focussed on ways to convert what we sell directly to the marketplace as quickly as possible into cash," says Danny Caswell, manager of Dell's asset management department. To do that, Dell went its own way, involving everyone from employees to suppliers to vendors to customers.

To determine improvements in return on invested capital, Dell's asset management team developed a set of internal benchmarks (Equation 10.2). Metrics included days sales outstanding (DSO), days in inventory (DSI), days payables outstanding (DPO). Add DSO and DSI, then subtract DPO, and you get the chief metric Dell uses to measure its liquidity: cash conversion cycle (CCC).

$$DSO + DSI - DPO = CCC \qquad (10.2)$$

The metrics tell a compelling tale. Dell's cash conversion cycle went from an acceptable 40 days to a phenomenal minus 5 days in the fourth quarter of 1997. "Our biggest improvement was in the inventory area, which we drove down from 30-plus days to 13 days," Caswell says. "We analysed key inventory drivers to identify who was holding inventory and where. It turned out to be us almost exclusively."

## 7 AND 8. PREPARE A CASH FLOW WORKSHEET, DETAILING MONTHLY RECEIPTS AND EXPENSES. EXTEND THE WORKSHEET INTO A MONTHLY CASH FLOW FORECAST AND THEN PREPARE THREE-YEAR ANNUALIZED FORECASTS ON CASH FLOWS USING THE TEMPLATE PROVIDED IN CHAPTER 3

As well as managing historic cash flows, planning for future liquidity is essential on the part of any corporate. Cash flow forecasting will require little introduction to most business persons. It's easy for the bank or equity investor to say "Please prepare a cash forecast for the next 12 months." However, the compilation of the document can be a long and arduous process.

All businesses must, of course, preserve liquidity in order to meet cash commitments to the creditors, employees, and shareholders. A good forward order book will be useless if there isn't the cash needed to finance the production of a firm's products. The ability, therefore, to be able to forecast cash movements and then monitor progress is a key requirement in business planning.

A good place to start is by completing a cash flow worksheet (see Table 3.2 in Chapter 2). If your company sells mainly on credit, then the analysis of collections will be of crucial importance. However, if you are selling mainly for cash, then more focus will be needed on disbursements. It's a question of fully analyzing the cash profile of your business and committing it to the worksheet.

The example is shown for a small business HRT and payments and receipts have been estimated for the year on a detailed monthly summary basis. The closing balance varies between a debit and credit position.

## 9. RUN SOME SENSITIVITY ANALYSIS ON THE RESULTING CASH FLOWS TO SEE WHAT FLEXING CAN ACHIEVE AN IMPROVED END CASH FLOW POSITION – IS THE BUSINESS A CASH GENERATOR OR CASH CONSUMER?

For example, what if sales are 10% less or if overhead costs increase by 20%? Run these tests through to see the effect on resulting cash flows.

## 10. CALCULATE CASH FLOW GENERATION RATIOS – CAN YOU FINANCE ANY PREDICTED CASH SHORTFALLS?

The following four ratios (expressed as equations) should yield useful data to help us manage our cash flows, particularly if compared with long-term average values from peer group companies in the sector of the business being examined. As cash flow statements are a relatively novel phenomena, there is limited data available to make comparisons against. It will, therefore, probably be necessary for you to extract the information yourself from peer group performers.

The ratio in Equation 10.3 looks at the cash generated as a percentage of sales and can be used as an effective forecasting tool.

Operating cash flow to sales %

$$= \text{Operating cash flow/Total sales} \qquad (10.3)$$

The ratio in Equation 10.4 compares the cash generated from operations with the total investment in the business – hence we can monitor how effectively we are utilizing our cash investments.

Operating cash flow to operating assets %

$$= \text{Operating cash flow/Operating assets} \qquad (10.4)$$

This is the cash flow equivalent of operating profit to operating assets, but should be higher as operating profit is stated after depreciation, whereas operating cash flow ignores depreciation. Again, this is a ratio to compare with competitors and sector norms.

The ratio in Equation 10.5 looks at the net cash flow returns on a free cash flow basis that are being achieved on sales. This again will be a useful tool in forecasting added value.

Free cash flow to sales % = Free cash flow/Total sales $\qquad (10.5)$

The ratio in Equation 10.6 has no direct comparative in the profit and loss account. It allows us to compare the net cash generation from the business before financing costs with the operating assets.

Free cash flow to operating assets %

$$= \text{Free cash flow/Operating assets} \times 100 \qquad (10.6)$$

## Capital intensity analysis

The following ratios (again expressed as equations) can be used to examine the nature of the capital investment in the business. Two of the ratios are derived from the balance sheet. They are included here as they form part of the overall analysis.

The ratio in Equation 10.7 tells us whether the business is investing at a rate higher than the depreciation charge or not. A result under 1 shows the business may be underinvesting. A result over 1.5 shows the business is investing aggressively and this should reflect in the growth rates being achieved.

Gross capex to total annual $\times$ depreciation

$$= \text{Gross capex/Total annual depreciation} \qquad (10.7)$$

In a capital-intensive business, we would expect a low value as the business has to continually invest substantial amounts of capital each year in order to remain competitive. In a low-capital business we would expect higher values. The ratio in Equation 10.8 gives us some indication whether the cash generation of the business is sufficient to increase the capex, should this be necessary for competitive reasons. It is only indicative because the business also has to service capital providers from the free cash flow.

Free cash flow to gross capex$\times$ = Free cash flow/Gross capex (10.8)

# Frequently Asked Questions (FAQs)

**Q1: Why is strategic cash flow management important?**
A: See Chapter 1.

**Q2: What items will feature in the capital cycle?**
A: See Chapter 2.

**Q3: What is the meaning of the cash conversion cycle?**
A: See Chapter 7 – Case study 1.

**Q4: How can I improve my receivables management?**
A: See Chapter 7 – Case study 1.

**Q5: How can I evaluate alternative investments?**
A: See Chapter 7 – Strategic cash flow management and capital investment.

**Q6: When should I use discounting cash flows?**
A: See Chapter 7 – Strategic cash flow management and capital investment.

**Q7: My bankers are including a cash flow coverage ratio in my loan documentation – how is this calculated?**

A: See Chapter 6.

**Q8: How do I compare differing international methods of cash flow presentation?**

A: See Chapter 5.

**Q9: Why does profit not equal cash flow?**

A: See Chapter 6.

**Q10: How do I set about preparing a cash flow statement?**

A: See Chapter 7.

# Index

ABC Hotel   67-78, 79-81
*Accounting for Life* (Benson)   34
accounting policies   94
acquisition   94
AG Barr plc   78-84, 122
annual accounts   16, 26, 27, 115
appraisal methods   84-8
articles   113-15
asset conversion cycle   10
auditing   26
average rate of return   85

balance sheets   16, 48-9, 60, 94
Banham, Russ   64, 122
bankruptcy   18-19
benchmarks   64-5
Benson, Lord   34
best practice   29, 65-6
books   113-15
business life cycle   50-53
business performance   2-3

capital   11-12, 22
   cycle   117, 119-20
   intensity analysis   60-61, 126
   investment   84-8
   repayments   56-8
capital expenditure (capex)   12, 22
   practice   78, 84

state of the art   46-7, 50-53, 60-61
ten steps   122, 126
Carsberg, Bryan   34
case studies
   ABC Hotel   67-78, 79-81
   AG Barr plc   78-84
   Dell Computer Corporation   64-6
   JN Nichols (Vimto) plc   78-84
cash conversion cycle (CCC)   22, 65,
   94, 117, 122-3
cash flow   2-3, 44-7
   additional management   88-91
   analysis   47-58
   coverage ratios   67
   patterns   53-6, 58
*The Cash Flow Management Book for
   Non-Profits* (Dropkin)   100
cash flow statements   3-42, 48
   electronic publication   26-7
   key concepts   94
   practice   82-3
   state of the art   58-9
   ten steps   117
cash flow worksheets   20, 22-3, 28,
   117-19, 124
*Cash is Still King* (Checkley)   100-101
cash plan online (CPO)   28
*Cashflow Control* (Graham)   100

*Cashflow Forecasting and Liquidity*
  (Graham)   100
Caswell, Danny   64-5, 123
Checkley, Keith   100-101
Coca-Cola   78, 122
Companies Act   26
comparisons   27, 59, 78-84, 117-19,
  122
competition   27, 49, 60, 70
  practice   78-84
  ten steps   117, 119, 122
construction budgets   71, 72-3
Consultancy (PVT) Ltd   68
contingent liabilities   95
counterclaims   90
County NatWest   3
covenants   67, 71
credit   12, 18, 44
  customer   12
  key concepts   95
  practice   90-91
customer viability   27

*Daily Telegraph*   2, 5-7
days payables outstanding (DPO)
  64-5, 123
days sales in inventory (DSI)   64-5, 123
days sales outstanding (DSO)   64-5,
  123
debt   27, 44, 48-9, 57
  analysis ratios   61
  capacity   11
  key concepts   95
  practice   89
  repayment   67
  service   22, 71, 77
decline period   22, 52-3
deferred liabilities   95
definitions   9-13
Dell Computer Corporation   64-6,
  122-3
Deloitte & Touche Consulting Group   5
direct method   17-18, 117, 119, 121
discounting formula   86, 96

dividends   10, 22, 46, 49
  key concepts   96
  practice   67, 78
  ten steps   122
Dropkin, Murray   100
Du Pont formula   16-17, 117, 119,
  120-21

e-dimension   25-31
e-learning   29-31, 119
e-trading   26
earnings before interest, tax,
  depreciation, and amortization
  (EBITDA)   71, 96
electronic publication   26-7
estimation techniques   96
evolution   15-24
Excel   67, 68, 71
*Export Today*   30, 110

factoring agreements   89
Falconer, Lord   5
filters   28
finance   78, 122
Financial Accounting Standards Board
  (FASB)   11, 17, 121
Financial Reporting Standard (FRS) No.
  1 – Cash Flow Statements   11, 16,
  34-41, 44-7
*Financial Times*   2-3, 104
financing   13, 47
Finland   34
forecasting   16, 19-20, 21-3
  e-dimension   28
  state of the art   59
  ten steps   117, 119, 124
France   4
France Telecom   4
free cash flow   49
frequently asked questions (FAQs)
  127-8

Gahlon, James M.   99
gearing   52, 56-8, 96-7

generally accepted accounting
   principles (GAAP)   34
Germany   4
global dimension   33-42
Global Payment Systems   30
glossary   94-9
Graham, Alastair   100
growth period   21, 51-3, 55-8, 61

*Harvard Business Review*   29-30, 106
Hayden, Allyson   100
historic cash flow   16, 117-19, 121,
   124
hotel project   67-78, 79-81

*The Independent*   2, 4
indirect method   17-18, 117-19, 121
interest   22, 46, 56-8, 68, 71
internal rate of return (IRR)   86-7, 97
International Accounting Standard (IAS)
   No. 7 - Cash Flow Statements   11,
   16, 34-41
International Accounting Standards
   Committee (IASC)   34, 42
international accounting standards (IAS)
   26-7, 34-41
Internet   26, 29, 31
intranets   26, 27
investment   13, 16, 44-7, 60
   key concepts   97
   practice   84-6
   project finance   67-78
Irn Bru   78, 122

James, David   7
JN Nichols (Vimto) plc   78-84, 122
joint stock companies   16

key aspects
   concepts   93-9
   frequently asked questions   127-8
   glossary   94-9
   information   47
   resources   103-15

ten steps   117-26
thinkers   93, 99-101
knowledge base   27-9

land values   70
liquidity   64, 97, 123
long-term forecasting   21-3
Lotus   67

machine installations   87-8
maturity period   21-2, 52, 53-5
Meredith, Tom   64, 122-3
Millennium Central Ltd   5
Millennium Commission   5-6
Millennium Dome   4-7
Millennium system   28
model-making   67-8, 71-8
Murray, Malcolm Jr   18

negative cash flow   10, 21-2
net capital expenditure (net capex)
   46-7
net cash inflow   44, 47, 49-50
net present value   85-6
New Millennium Experience Company
   (NMEC)   5-7
Nokia   34
NTL   4

O'Connor, Mike   5
operations   12, 44, 49, 74-7

payback   84-5, 87
performance ratios   59
periodicals   103-13
Polly Peck   3-4
practice   63-91
preferential credit   90-91
press   103-13
PricewaterhouseCoopers   6
profit and loss accounts   16, 58, 98
profitability index   86
project finance   67-78
Pyne, Joe   31

Quarmby, David   6

ratio analysis   17, 67, 71, 77
    calculation   125-6
    debt analysis   61
    performance   59
recession   2
reporting   44-7
research and development   10
reservation of title   89-90
resources   28-9, 103-15
return on assets (ROA)   17
return on capital employed (ROCE)   85
revaluation reserve   98
Richmond Software   28
risk   67, 68, 84
Robert Morris Associates   18
Romalpa terms   89

Scotland   78, 122
sensitivity analysis   71-2, 118-19, 124
shortfalls   118-19, 125-6
soft drinks industry   78-84, 122
software   67-8, 71
start-ups   50-51
state of the art   43-61
Statement of Financial Accounting
    Standards No. 95 – Statement of Cash
    Flows   17, 34-41, 121
stock   12, 44, 49, 89-90
stock market   2-3
*Strategic Finance*   30-31, 111-12
Sun Microsystems   64, 122
supplier credit   12
sustainability   58
Switzerland   4

taxation   10, 13, 18, 22
    deferred   95
    practice   78, 84
    state of the art   46, 50-56
    ten steps   122
techniques   27, 119
ten steps   117-26
time value of money   85-6
tools   27, 119
tourism   69
TranSettlements Network   28
*The Treasurer*   107-8, 112

uniform credit analysis (UCA)   18, 121
Uniform Electronic Transactions Act
    30
Unilever   30
United Kingdom (UK)   2-3, 4, 16
    e-dimension   26
    global dimension   34-41
    practice   78
    state of the art   46
United Parcel Service (UPS)   31
United States (US)   16-17, 34-41,
    64-6, 99
University of Minnesota   99

valuations   70-71
Vigeland, Robert L.   99
Vimto   78-84, 122

*Wall Street Journal*   104
Websites   26-31, 117, 119, 122
working capital cycle   66

yield   86-7

Printed and bound by CPI Group (UK) Ltd, Croydon, CR0 4YY

13/04/2025

14656558-0004